FROM DEMOCRACY'S ROOTS TO A COUNTRY DIVIDED

AMERICA FROM 1816 TO 1850

FROM DEMOCRACY'S ROOTS TO A COUNTRY DIVIDED

AMERICA FROM 1816 TO 1850

EDITED BY JEFF WALLENFELDT, MANAGER, GEOGRAPHY AND HISTORY

Britannica®
Educational Publishing

IN ASSOCIATION WITH

ROSEN
EDUCATIONAL SERVICES

Published in 2012 by Britannica Educational Publishing
(a trademark of Encyclopædia Britannica, Inc.)
in association with Rosen Educational Services, LLC
29 East 21st Street, New York, NY 10010.

Distributed exclusively by Rosen Educational Services.
For a listing of additional Britannica Educational Publishing titles, call toll free (800) 237-9932.

First Edition

Britannica Educational Publishing
Michael I. Levy: Executive Editor
Marilyn L. Barton: Senior Coordinator, Production Control
Steven Bosco: Director, Editorial Technologies
Lisa S. Braucher: Senior Producer and Data Editor
Yvette Charboneau: Senior Copy Editor
Kathy Nakamura: Manager, Media Acquisition
Jeff Wallenfeldt, Manager, Geography and History

Rosen Educational Services
Shalini Saxena: Editor
Nelson Sá: Art Director
Cindy Reiman: Photography Manager
Karen Huang: Photo Research
Matthew Cauli: Cover Design
Brian Garvey: Designer
Introduction by Jeff Wallenfeldt

Library of Congress Cataloging-in-Publication Data

From democracy's roots to a country divided : America from 1816 to 1850 / edited by Jeff Wallenfeldt.—1st ed.
    p. cm.—(Documenting America : the primary source documents of a nation)
"In association with Britannica Educational Publishing, Rosen Educational Services."
Includes bibliographical references and index.
ISBN 978-1-61530-674-9 (library binding)
1. United States—History—1815-1861. 2. United States—History—1815-1816—Sources. I. Wallenfeldt, Jeffrey H.
E338.F86 2012
973.5—dc23

2011024840

Manufactured in the United States of America

On the cover: *American Progress,* chromolithograph print, c. 1873, after an 1872 painting of the same title by John Gast. The
image portrays westward-traveling settlers and the incipient railway and telegraph networks that helped fuel the idea of the
American manifest destiny. *Library of Congress, Washington, D.C. (digital id: ppmsca 09855).* Monroe Doctrine. *Records of the
U.S. Senate, National Archives, Washington, D.C.*

On pages 1, 9, 19, 32, 39, 49, 60: The town of Lockport, New York sits on the Erie Canal. Canals and other developments in transportation in the first half of the 19th century helped unite distant regions of the country and facilitated the nation's commerce. © *Hulton
Archive/Getty Images*

CONTENTS

3

23

25

40

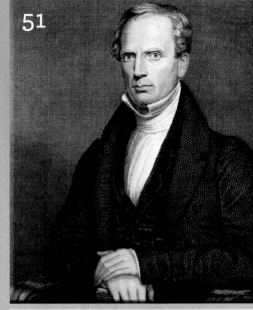

51

55

INTRODUCTION

History tells us not only who we were but helps us to understand who we are today and how we got here. The historian acts as a guide and interpreter, leading the student of history on carefully chosen routes through the past. Often the road is well-traveled, with predictable stops at familiar landmarks where the student hears stories so summarily handed down that they fail to register. The history student takes a mental photo without thinking, the equivalent of a glossy postcard. A date is memorized, along with some names, a place, and a catchphrase. This is history as package tourism. There is so much more to be gained.

The challenge for the historian is to present new perspectives, to look again, and in a different light, at events in an attempt to understand them better and bring them to life. The challenge for the student is not to be a passive tourist but an active adventurer through history, engaging and experiencing it. There is no better way to do this than to immerse oneself in primary source documents—in the unfiltered words of those who made history. By interspersing a selection of revealing primary sources in a narrative account, this volume offers the opportunity to do just that for the period of American history between 1816 and 1850. Presenting a description and analysis of the period, its events, and its issues, the narrative provides a framework for approaching these documents that allows the reader to make sense of them, and ultimately, of the period itself. When these documents are short, they are presented whole with the running text of the narrative; more often, excerpts are provided that give a flavour of the document, which is presented more fully in the Appendix. Specific introductions for each document provide additional context.

In the period immediately after the War of 1812, Americans, pleased to have survived again against the mighty British, enjoyed an interlude of national bonhomie that became known as the Era of Good Feelings. The country grew with the acquisition of Florida from Spain in 1819 and flexed its foreign policy muscles in 1823 with the pronouncement of the Monroe Doctrine. Much influenced by Secretary of State John Quincy Adams, this policy declaration made clear that the United States would not brook European intervention in the affairs of the Western Hemisphere, a bold statement by a country that was relatively weak compared with the European empires. As the United States staked its place in the world, Americans were very much involved in shaping the nature of their society. The Supreme Court, guided by Chief Justice John Marshall, played a pivotal role in this process with a series of landmark decisions, not the least of which was *Dartmouth College* v. *Woodward* (1819), which freed corporations from

A view of Lower Manhattan and New York Harbour in the early 19th century. Imagno/Hulton Archive/Getty Images

state inference, establishing a business-friendly foundation that became the bulwark of American capitalism.

In 1820, slavery, arguably the most divisive institution in American society, came to the fore as Missouri sought to join the Union as a slave state. Ultimately, Missouri and Maine (a free state) gained statehood together as a result of the Missouri Compromise engineered by Henry Clay, thereby retaining the balance between slave and non-slave states. Adams's response to the Compromise, recorded in his diary, says much about the complexity of the conflict: "The bargain between freedom and slavery contained in the Constitution of the United States is morally and politically vicious, inconsistent with the principles upon which alone our Revolution can be justified...and grossly unequal and impolitic, by admitting that slaves are at once enemies to be kept in subjection, property to be secured or restored to their owners, and persons not be represented themselves, but for whom their masters are privileged with nearly a double share of representation."

The slavery-based, export-driven agricultural economy of the South and burgeoning manufacturing economy of the Northeast were at loggerheads. Clay saw a solution to this problem and an important source of federal revenue in the introduction of a tariff on foreign goods that would create a domestic market for a self-sufficient American System in which industry could prosper. "No one of these interests is felt in the same degree and cherished with the same solicitude throughout all parts of the Union," he said in defending the tariff before Congress in 1824. "But all these great interests are confided to the protection of one government...If we prosper and are happy, protection must be extended to all." The integration of the country through improvements to the transportation network that included canal, road, and railroad building and the proliferation of steamboats also was an important component of American industrialization. As industrialism grew, its influence on American life became evident in a variety of ways, including the increasing prevalence of factories, such as the Lowell Cotton Mills in Massachusetts. After visiting the mills in 1834, frontiersman-turned-congressman Davy Crockett observed that the well-dressed, lively, and genteel single girls who worked there (and who were provided with housing) "looked as if they were coming from a quilting frolic." Their apparent contentment would be relatively short-lived, however, for women millworkers in New England would be among the first American labourers to organize.

Their discontent was mirrored by Thomas Skidmore, the leader of the New York Workingman's Party, who in 1829 called for education reform and decried the inequality of wealth and property in the country, demanding, "Feed first the hungry; clothe first the naked or ill-clad; provide comfortable homes for all by hewing down colossal estates among us and equalizing all property; take care that the animal wants be supplied first... then you will have a good field and good subjects for education." The extension of education to women, especially in the growing cities, brought new opportunities to women such as Catharine Beecher, who asked, also in 1829, why society would task a woman with the responsibility for the physical and moral well-being of her family without providing formal instruction in "at least some of the general principles of that perfect and wonderful piece of mechanism committed to her preservation and care?" Later in the century, the Seneca Falls Convention, organized by Elizabeth Cady Stanton and Lucretia Mott in 1848, would issue a declaration that stated, "Now, in view of this entire disenfranchisement of one-half the people of this country, their social and religious degradation...and because women do feel themselves aggrieved, oppressed, and fraudulently deprived of their most sacred rights, we insist that they have immediate admission to all the rights and privileges which belong to them as citizens of the United States."

Even before women demanded the vote, that same privilege was sought by property-less men, who also had been denied the franchise. Their case was made eloquently to the Virginia Convention in 1829 by John Marshall, who noted that "landless citizens have been ignominiously driven from the polls" in times of peace but "generously summoned, in war, to the battlefield." "Virtue, intelligence are not among the products of soil," he said.

"Attachment to property, often a sordid sentiment, is not to be confounded with the sacred flame of patriotism." As the 1820s progressed, property restrictions on voting were finally removed in most states.

When Andrew Jackson, the hero of the War of 1812's Battle of New Orleans, was elected president, it was widely seen as a triumph for the rank and file, the beginning of the "Era of the Common Man." But just how much Jacksonian democracy was actually an assault on privilege depended on the locality and the circumstances. Jackson himself was very wealthy; however, his brain trust adeptly presented him as a man of the people and the Democratic Party as an agent of populist change. Certainly Washington, D.C. society doyenne Mrs. Samuel Harrison Smith saw Jackson as a man of the people and was outraged by those who descended upon the White House to celebrate the inauguration of Jackson in 1829. In a letter to a friend, she wrote, "The majesty of the people had disappeared" to be replaced by "a rabble, a mob, of boys, Negroes, women, children—scrambling, fighting, romping."

Whatever Jackson's true feelings were about the common people, his attitude toward Native Americans was much less complex. He saw them as an impediment to "the waves of population and civilization rolling westward." "What good man would prefer a country covered with forests and ranged by a few thousand savages to our extensive republic, studded with cities, towns, and prosperous farms...and filled with all the blessings of liberty, civilization, and religion?" Jackson asked. Indian removal was necessary, Jackson argued, so that there would be no conflict between the federal and state governments regarding authority over the Native Americans. When a federal-state dispute did arise with South Carolina's attempted nullification of an 1832 tariff, Jackson steadfastly opposed the state's rights claimed by John C. Calhoun in saying that it was the "original and inherent obligation of the states to protect their citizens" and "the most sacred of all their duties to watch over and resist the encroachments of government."

As expansion westward continued, many began to covet Mexican land in the West. Americans who had settled in Texas fought for and gained their independence from Mexico and established a sovereign republic in 1836. During the presidencies of John Tyler (1841–45) and James K. Polk (184–49), interest grew in annexing Texas (accomplished in 1845), in acquiring the Oregon Territory that was claimed by both the United States and Britain, and in pushing U.S. borders ever westward. In 1845, editor John L. O'Sullivan encapsulated this desire when he wrote that it was the "manifest destiny" of the United States to "overspread the continent allotted by Providence for the free development of our yearly multiplying millions." A military provocation of ambiguous origin provided the rationalization for war with Mexico (1846–48), the winning of which netted the United States huge expanses of formerly Mexican territory and helped to make good on Sullivan's prediction that 250 or 300 million Americans were "destined to gather beneath the flutter of the stripes and stars, in the fast hastening year of the Lord 1945!"

At the same time that the country was growing in size and military power, American arts and culture were increasingly staking a claim to importance and uniqueness. American literature made its mark in the works of James Fenimore Cooper, Nathaniel Hawthorne, Ralph Waldo Emerson, John Greenleaf Whittier, Edgar Allen Poe, and Henry Wadsworth Longfellow, and James Russell Lowell. Lowell called for the pursuit of a national literature, writing, "We would no longer see the spirit of our people held up as a mirror to the Old World; but rather lying like one of our own inland oceans, reflecting not only the mountain and the rock, the forest and the red man, but also the steamboat and the railcar, the cornfield and factory."

The push-and-pull tension between nationalism and sectionalism that had been evident throughout the first half of the 19th century heated up in the wake of the Mexican War as the matter of slavery and the future of its extension into the country's newly acquired territory became the great issue of the day. Abolitionism was only one of many reform movements that had experienced an upsurge in the previous decades, but as the era moved to a close, the discussion of slavery became more and more central to the national dialogue. Some abolitionists looked toward a measured elimination of the institution; others, such as William Lloyd Garrison, publisher of *The Liberator*, were out of patience. As early as 1831, Garrison recanted his advocacy of "the popular but pernicious doctrine of gradual abolition." "Tell a man whose house is on fire to give a moderate alarm...tell the mother to gradually extricate her babe from the fire into which it has fallen," Garrison wrote. At the opposite extreme were those who saw great advantage to the continuation of slavery and to its proliferation in the newly acquired territories and who argued that the Founding Fathers had been on their side. "When these new states come into the Union, they are controlled by the Constitution only.," said an editorial 1847. "And as that instrument permits slavery in all the states that are parties to it, how can Congress prevent it?" Despite earlier compromises and the increasing integration of the economy, the divide that was widening over that question would come to define the character of the era to come and split the country in two.

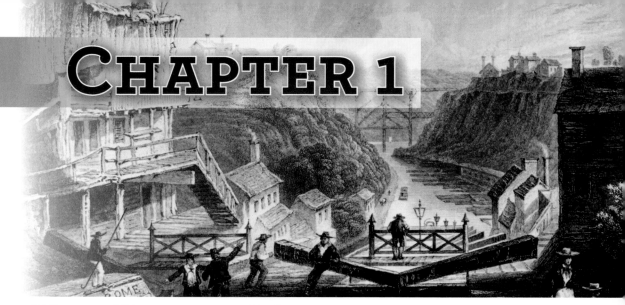

CHAPTER 1

THE ERA OF MIXED FEELINGS

The years between the election to the presidency of James Monroe in 1816 and of John Quincy Adams in 1824 have long been known in American history as the Era of Good Feelings. The phrase was conceived by a Boston editor during Monroe's visit to New England early in his first term. That a representative of the heartland of Federalism could speak in such positive terms of the visit by a Southern president—whose decisive election had marked not only a sweeping Republican victory but also the demise of the national Federalist Party—was dramatic testimony that former foes were inclined to put aside the sectional and political differences of the past.

EFFECTS OF THE WAR OF 1812

Later scholars have questioned the strategy and tactics of the United States in the War of 1812, the war's tangible results, and even the wisdom of commencing it in the first place. To contemporary Americans, however, the striking naval victories and Andrew Jackson's victory over the British at New Orleans created a reservoir of "good feeling" on which Monroe was able to draw.

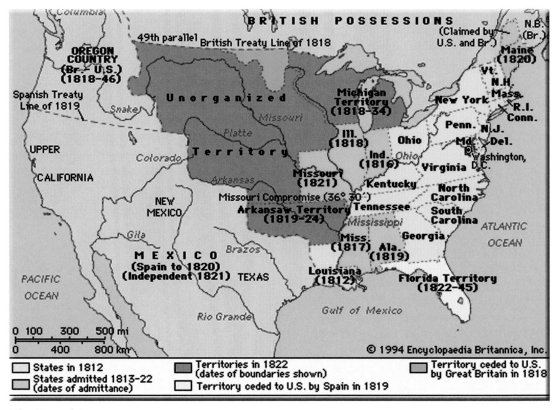

The United States, 1812–22.

Abetting the mood of nationalism was the foreign policy of the United States after the war. Florida was acquired from Spain (1819) in negotiations, the success of which owed more to Jackson's indifference to such niceties as the inviolability of foreign borders and to the country's evident readiness to back him up than it did to diplomatic finesse. Additionally, the Monroe Doctrine (1823), actually a few phrases inserted in a long presidential message, declared that the United States would not become involved in European affairs and would not accept European interference in the Americas; its immediate effect on other nations was slight, and that on its own citizenry was impossible to gauge, yet its self-assured tone in warning off the Old World from the New reflected well the nationalist mood that swept the country.

Internally, the decisions of the Supreme Court under Chief Justice John Marshall in such cases as *McCulloch* v. *Maryland* (1819) and *Gibbons* v. *Ogden* (1824) promoted nationalism by strengthening Congress and national power at the expense of the states. The congressional decision to charter the second Bank of the United States (1816) was explained in part by the country's financial weaknesses,

James Monroe. Buyenlarge/Archive Photos/Getty Images

Document: James Monroe: The Monroe Doctrine (1823)

The Monroe Doctrine comprised some general remarks on foreign policy that Pres. James Monroe included in his annual message to Congress on Dec. 2, 1823. The first draft of the message included a reproof of the French for their invasion of Spain, an acknowledgment of Greek independence in the revolt against Turkey, and some further indications of American concern in European affairs. Secretary of State John Quincy Adams argued for the better part of two days against such expressions, which were finally eliminated from the message. "The ground that I wish to take," Adams noted in his diary, "is that of earnest remonstrance against the interference of the European powers by force in South America, but to disclaim all interference on our part with Europe; to make an American cause, and adhere inflexibly to that." Despite the ambiguities that have surrounded the application of this policy since its inception, one theme was clear: there were two worlds, the Old and the New; each must lead its separate existence, always aware of a bond between them, but never intervene in the affairs of the other.

A precise knowledge of our relations with foreign powers as respects our negotiations and transactions with each is thought to be particularly necessary....

At the proposal of the Russian Imperial government, made through the minister of the emperor residing here, full power and instructions have been transmitted to the minister of the United States at St. Petersburg to arrange by amicable negotiation the respective rights and interests of the two nations on the northwest coast of this continent. A similar proposal had been made by His Imperial Majesty to the government of Great Britain, which has likewise been acceded to. The government of the United States has been desirous, by this friendly proceeding, of manifesting the great value which they have invariably attached to the friendship of the emperor and their solicitude to cultivate the best understanding with his government.

In the discussions to which this interest has given rise and in the arrangements by which they may terminate the occasion has been judged proper for asserting, as a principle in which the rights and interests of the United States are involved, that the American continents, by the free and independent condition which they have assumed and maintain, are henceforth not to be considered as subjects for future colonization by any European powers....

exposed by the War of 1812, and in part by the intrigues of financial interests. The readiness of Southern Jeffersonians—former strict constructionists—to support such a measure indicates, too, an amazing degree of nationalist feeling. Perhaps the clearest sign of a new sense of national unity was the victorious Republican Party, standing in solitary splendour on the national political horizon, its long-time foes the Federalists vanished without a trace (on the national level) and Monroe, the Republican standard-bearer, reelected so overwhelmingly in 1820 that it was long believed that the one electoral vote denied him had been held back only in order to preserve Washington's record of unanimous selection.

NATIONAL DISUNITY

For all the signs of national unity and feelings of oneness, equally convincing evidence points in the opposite direction. The very Supreme Court decisions that delighted friends of strong national government infuriated its opponents, while Marshall's defense of the rights of private property was construed by critics as betraying a predilection for one kind of property over another.

Document: John Marshall: *Dartmouth College* v. *Woodward* (1819)

Daniel Webster's famous speech defending Dartmouth College before the Supreme Court in Dartmouth College v. Woodward *is said to have brought tears to the eyes of Chief Justice John Marshall. Marshall's majority opinion in favour of the college was not based on sentiment but rather on his strong views concerning the contract clause in the Constitution. He had previously set forth the principle in* Fletcher v. Peck *that contracts could not be impaired by state rulings. In the* Dartmouth *case he extended this principle to corporate charters such as the one at hand. This new doctrine was to be a turning point in constitutional law. Since business corporations were now free from state interference, investors were more willing to support such enterprises. Thus, the whole field of business was encouraged to expand, with far-reaching effects on the American economy. Half a century later, Justice Samuel Miller remarked that "it may be doubted whether any decision ever delivered by any court has had such a pervading operation and influence in controlling legislation as this."*

It can require no argument to prove that the circumstances of this case constitute a contract. An application is made to the Crown for a charter to incorporate a religious and literary institution. In the application it is stated that large contributions have been made for the object, which will be conferred on the corporation as soon as it shall be created. The charter is granted, and on its faith the property is conveyed. Surely in this transaction every ingredient of a complete and legitimate contract is to be found.

The points for consideration are:

• Is this contract protected by the Constitution of the United States?
• Is it impaired by the acts under which the defendant holds?

On the first point, it has been argued that the word "contract," in its broadest sense, would comprehend the political relations between the government and its citizens, would extend to offices held within a state for state purposes and to many of those laws concerning civil institutions, which must change with circumstances and be modified by ordinary legislation; which deeply concern the public, and which, to preserve good government, the public judgment must control — that even marriage is a contract, and its obligations are affected by the laws respecting divorces; that the clause in the Constitution, if construed in its greatest latitude, would prohibit these laws....

The growth of the West, encouraged by the conquest of Indian lands during the War of 1812, was by no means regarded as an unmixed blessing. Eastern conservatives sought to keep land prices high; speculative interests opposed a policy that would be advantageous to poor squatters; politicians feared a change in the sectional balance of power; and businessmen were wary of a new section with interests unlike their own. European visitors testified that, even during the so-called Era of Good Feelings, Americans characteristically expressed scorn for their countrymen in sections other than their own.

Economic hardship, especially the financial panic of 1819, also created disunity. The causes of the panic were complex, but its greatest effect was clearly the tendency of its victims to blame it on one or another hostile or malevolent interest—whether the second Bank of the United States, Eastern capitalists, selfish speculators, or perfidious politicians—each charge expressing the bad feeling that existed side by side with the good.

If harmony seemed to reign on the level of national political parties, disharmony prevailed within the states. In the

Cotton plantations, while vital to the Southern economy, thrived on the inhumane exploitation of slave labour. The slavery issue divided the country for much of the 19th century. Hulton Archive/ Getty Images

early 19th-century United States, local and state politics were typically waged less on behalf of great issues than for petty gain. That the goals of politics were often sordid did not mean that political contests were bland. In every section, state factions led by shrewd men waged bitter political warfare to attain or entrench themselves in power.

The most dramatic manifestation of national division was the political struggle over slavery, particularly over its

Document: John Quincy Adams: Slavery and the Constitution (1820)

The complexity of the issues involved in the debate about the Missouri Compromise is revealed in the selection that appears below from the diary of John Quincy Adams, dated March 3, 1820, only three days before the Missouri Enabling Act went into effect. Pres. James Monroe had assembled his cabinet for advice before signing the bills admitting Maine and Missouri, and Secretary of State Adams recommended their acceptance. He did so despite the fact that he believed that slavery was a profound moral evil. At the same time, however, he was convinced that the Constitution did not give the federal government the power to abolish the institution. "The abolition of slavery where it is established must be left entirely to the people of the state itself," he declared in a letter of the same date to Gov. Jonathan Jennings of Indiana. "The healthy have no right to reproach or to prescribe for the diseased."

When I came this day to my office, I found there a note requesting me to call at one o'clock at the President's house. It was then one, and I immediately went over. He expected that the two bills — for the admission of Maine, and to enable Missouri to make a constitution — would have been brought to him for his signature, and he had summoned all the members of the administration to ask their opinions, in writing, to be deposited in the Department of State, upon two questions: (1) whether Congress had a constitutional right to prohibit slavery in a territory; and (2) whether the 8th Section of the Missouri bill (which interdicts slavery *forever* in the territory north of thirty-six and a half latitude) was applicable only to the territorial state, or could extend to it after it should become a state....

After this meeting, I walked home with Calhoun, who said that ... in the Southern country ... domestic labor was confined to the blacks; and such was the prejudice that if he, who was the most popular man in his district, were to keep a white servant in his house, his character and reputation would be irretrievably ruined.

I said that this confounding of the ideas of servitude and labor was one of the bad effects of slavery; but he thought it attended with many excellent consequences. It did not apply to all kinds of labor — not, for example, to farming. He himself had often held the plough; so had his father. Manufacturing and mechanical labor was not degrading. It was only manual labor — the proper work of slaves. No white person could descend to that. And it was the best guarantee to equality among the whites. It produced an unvarying level among them. It not only did not excite but did not even admit of inequalities, by which one white man could domineer over another....

spread into new territories. The Missouri Compromise of 1820 eased the threat of further disunity, at least for the time being. The sectional balance between the states was preserved: in the Louisiana Purchase, with the exception of the Missouri Territory, slavery was to be confined to the area south of the 36°30′ line.

Yet this compromise did not end the crisis but only postponed it.

The determination by Northern and Southern senators not to be outnumbered by one another suggests that the people continued to believe in the conflicting interests of the various great geographic sections. The weight of evidence indicates that the decade after the Battle of New Orleans was not an era of good feelings so much as one of mixed feelings.

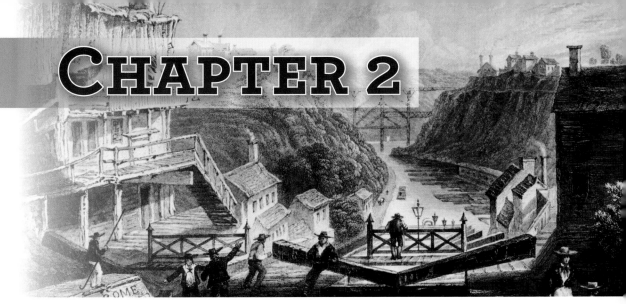

CHAPTER 2

THE ECONOMY

The American economy expanded and matured at a remarkable rate in the decades after the War of 1812. The rapid growth of the West created a great new centre for the production of grains and pork, permitting the country's older sections to specialize in other crops. New processes of manufacture, particularly in textiles, not only accelerated an "industrial revolution" in the Northeast but also, by drastically enlarging the Northern market for raw materials, helped account for a boom in Southern cotton production. If by mid-century Southerners of European descent had come to regard slavery—on which the cotton economy relied—as a "positive good" rather than the "necessary evil" that they had earlier held the system to be, it was largely because of the increasingly central role played by cotton in earning profits for the region. Industrial workers organized the country's first trade unions and even workingmen's political parties early in the period. The corporate form thrived in an era of booming capital requirements, and older and simpler forms of attracting investment capital were rendered obsolete. Commerce became increasingly specialized, the division of labour in the disposal of goods for sale matching the increasingly sophisticated division of labour that had come to characterize production.

The management of the growing economy was inseparable from political conflict in the emerging United States. At the start the issue was between agrarians (represented by Jeffersonian Republicans) wanting a decentralized system of easy credit and an investing community looking for stability and profit in financial markets. This latter group, championed by Alexander Hamilton and the Federalists, won the first round with the establishment of the first Bank of the United States (1791), jointly owned by the government and private stockholders. It was the government's fiscal agent (or, financial representative), and it put the centre of gravity of the credit system in Philadelphia, its headquarters. Its charter expired in 1811, and the financial chaos that hindered procurement and mobilization during the ensuing War of 1812 demonstrated the importance of such centralization. Hence, even Jeffersonian Republicans were converted to acceptance of a second Bank of the United States, chartered in 1816.

The second Bank of the United States faced constant political fire, but the conflict now was not merely between farming and mercantile interests but

Wood engraving relating to the financial setback experienced on the U.S. frontier following the Panic of 1837. Library of Congress, Washington, D.C.

also between local bankers who wanted access to the profits of an expanding credit system and those who, like the president of the Bank of the United States, Nicholas Biddle, wanted more regularity and predictability in banking through top-down control. The Constitution gave the United States exclusive power to coin money but allowed for the chartering of banks by individual states, and these banks were permitted to issue notes that also served as currency. The state banks, whose charters were often political plums, lacked coordinated inspection and safeguards against risky loans usually collateralized by land, whose value fluctuated wildly, as did the value of the banknotes. Overspeculation, bankruptcies, contraction, and panics were the inevitable result.

Biddle's hope was that the large deposits of government funds in the Bank of the United States would allow it to become the major lender to local banks, and from that position of strength it could squeeze the unsound ones into either responsibility or extinction. But this notion ran afoul of the growing democratic spirit that insisted that the right to extend credit and choose its recipients was too precious to be confined to a wealthy elite. This difference of views produced the classic battle between Biddle and Pres. Andrew Jackson, culminating in Biddle's attempt to win recharter for the Bank of the United States, Jackson's veto and transfer of the government funds to pet banks, and the Panic of 1837. Not until the 1840s did the federal government place its funds in an independent treasury, and not until the Civil War was there legislation creating a national banking system. The country was strong enough to survive, but the politicization of making fiscal policy continued to be a major theme of American economic history.

TRANSPORTATION REVOLUTION

Improvements in transportation, a key to the advance of industrialization everywhere, were especially vital in the United States. A fundamental problem of the developing American economy was the great geographic extent of the country and the appallingly poor state of its roads. The broad challenge to weave the Great Lakes, Mississippi Valley, and Gulf and Atlantic coasts into a single national market was first met by putting steam to work on the rich network of navigable rivers. As early as 1787, John Fitch had demonstrated a workable steamboat to onlookers in Philadelphia; some years later, he repeated the feat in New York City. But it is characteristic of American history that, in the absence of governmental encouragement, private backing was needed to bring an invention into full play. As a result, popular credit for the first steamboat goes to Robert Fulton, who found the financing to make his initial Hudson River

Illustration of an early version of John Fitch's steamboat. Library of Congress, Washington, D.C.

run of the *Clermont* in 1807 more than a onetime feat. From that point forward, on inland waters, steam was king, and its most spectacular manifestation was the Mississippi River paddle wheeler, a unique creation of unsung marine engineers challenged to make a craft that could "work" in shallow swift-running waters. Their solution was to put cargo, engines, and passengers on a flat open deck above the waterline, which was possible in the mild climate of large parts of the drainage basin of the Father of Waters. The Mississippi River steamboat not only became an instantly recognizable American icon but also had an impact on the law. In the case of

Gibbons v. *Ogden* (1824), Chief Justice Marshall affirmed the exclusive right of the federal government to regulate traffic on rivers flowing between states.

Canals and railroads were not as distinctively American in origin as the paddle wheeler, but, whereas 18th-century canals in England and continental Europe were simple conveniences for moving bulky loads cheaply at low speed, Americans integrated the country's water transport system by connecting rivers flowing toward the Atlantic Ocean with the Great Lakes and the Ohio-Mississippi River valleys. The best-known conduit, the Erie Canal, connected the Hudson River to the Great Lakes, linking the West to the port of New York City. Other major canals in Pennsylvania, Maryland, and Ohio joined Philadelphia and Baltimore to the West via the Ohio River and its tributaries. Canal building was increasingly popular throughout the 1820s and '30s, sometimes financed by states or by a combination of state and private effort. But many overbuilt or unwisely begun canal projects collapsed, and states that were "burned" in the process became more wary of such ventures.

Canal development was overtaken by the growth of the railroads, which were far more efficient in covering the great distances underserved by the road system and indispensable in the trans-Mississippi West. Work on the Baltimore and Ohio line, the first railroad in the United States, was begun in 1828, and a great burst of construction boosted the country's rail network from zero to 30,000 miles (50,000 kilometres) by 1860. The financing alone, no less than the operation of the burgeoning system, had a huge political and economic impact. Adams was a decided champion of "national internal improvements"—the federally assisted development of turnpikes, lighthouses, and dredging and channel-clearing operations (that is, whatever it took to assist commerce). That term, however, was more closely associated with Henry Clay, like Adams a strong nationalist. Clay proposed an American System, which would, through internal improvements and the imposition of tariffs, encourage the growth of an industrial sector that exchanged manufactured goods for the products of U.S. agriculture, thus benefiting each section of the country.

Document: Henry Clay: The Protective Tariff (1824)

The Tariff of 1824 raised duties generally and increased the number of commodities that were subject to tax. Its passage was largely due to the efforts of Henry Clay, who was motivated by a dual purpose. First, in order to make the country economically independent, Clay felt that a high tariff was necessary to reduce foreign competition and thus to strengthen the domestic market. At the same time that the home market would be protected, the national government would gain a source of revenue that could be applied to the internal improvements that, in his view, were necessary. Second, as a candidate for the presidency, Clay hoped to win votes in the manufacturing states of the Northeast by his American System, in which the tariff was an essential element. He outlined his views and defended the tariff in a speech in Congress on March 31, 1824, from which the following is taken.

The policy of all Europe is adverse to the reception of our agricultural produce so far as it comes into collision with its own; and, under that limitation, we are absolutely forbid to enter their ports, except under circumstances which deprive them of all value as a steady market. The policy of all Europe rejects those great staples of our country which consist of objects of human subsistence. The policy of all Europe refuses to receive from us anything but those raw materials of smaller value, essential to their manufactures, to which they can give a higher value, with the exception of tobacco and rice, which they cannot produce. Even Great Britain, to which we are its best customer, and from which we receive nearly one half in value of our whole imports, will not take from us articles of subsistence produced in our country cheaper than can be produced in Great Britain. ...

Is this foreign market, so incompetent at present, and which, limited as its demands are, operates so unequally upon the productive labor of our country, likely to improve in future? If I am correct in the views which I have presented to the committee, it must become worse and worse. What can improve it? Europe will not abandon her own agriculture to foster ours. We may even anticipate that she will more and more enter into competition with us in the supply of the West India market....

But the passionate opposition of many agrarians to the costs and expanded federal control inherent in the program created one battlefield in the long contest between the Democratic and Whig parties that did not end until the triumph of Whig economic ideas in the Republican Party during the Civil War.

BEGINNINGS OF INDUSTRIALIZATION

Economic, social, and cultural history cannot easily be separated. The creation of the "factory system" in the United States was the outcome of interaction between several characteristically American forces: faith in the future, a generally welcoming attitude toward immigrants, an abundance of resources linked to a shortage of labour, and a hospitable view of innovation. The pioneering textile industry, for example, sprang from an alliance of invention, investment, and philanthropy. Moses

Brown (later benefactor of the College of Rhode Island, renamed Brown University in honour of his nephew Nicholas) was looking to invest some of his family's mercantile fortune in the textile business. New England wool and southern cotton were readily available, as was water power from Rhode Island's swiftly flowing rivers. All that was lacking to convert a handcraft industry into one that was machine-based was machinery itself; however, the new devices for spinning and weaving that were coming into use in England were jealously guarded there. But Samuel Slater, a young English mechanic who immigrated to the United States in 1790 carrying the designs for the necessary machinery in his prodigious memory, became aware of Brown's ambitions and of the problems he was having with his machinery. Slater formed a partnership with Brown and others to reproduce the crucial equipment and build prosperous Rhode Island fabric factories.

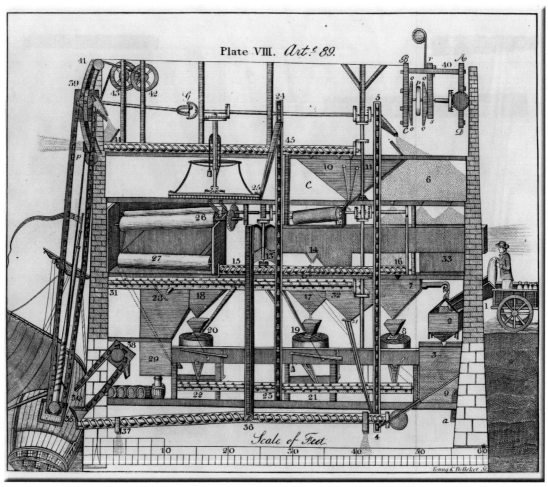

One of the first U.S. patents granted was to Oliver Evans in 1790 for his automatic gristmill. The mill produced flour from grain in a continuous process that required only one labourer to set the mill in motion. Library of Congress, Washington, D.C.

Local American inventive talent embodied in sometimes self-taught engineers was available, too. One conspicuous example was Delaware's Oliver Evans, who built a totally automatic flour mill in the 1780s and later founded a factory that produced steam engines; another was the ultimate Connecticut Yankee, Eli Whitney, who not only fathered the cotton gin but built a factory for mass producing muskets by fitting together interchangeable parts on an assembly line. Whitney got help from a supportive U.S. Army, which sustained him with advances on large procurement contracts. Such governmental support

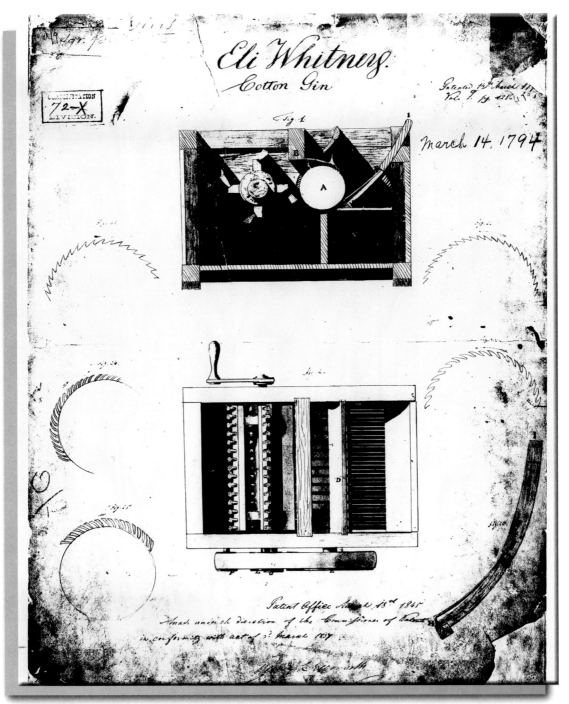

Sketch submitted to the Patent Office by Eli Whitney, showing the operation of the cotton gin.
National Archives, Washington, D.C.

of industrial development was rare, but, when it occurred, it was a crucial if often understated element in the industrializing of America.

Francis Cabot Lowell, who opened a textile factory in 1811 in the Massachusetts town later named for him, played a pathbreaking role as a paternalistic model employer. Whereas Slater and Brown used local families, living at home, to provide "hands" for their factories, Lowell brought in young women from the countryside and put them up in boardinghouses adjacent to the mills. The "girls"—most of them in or just out of their teens—were happy to be paid a few dollars for 60-hour workweeks that were less taxing than those they put in as farmers' daughters. Their moral behaviour was supervised by matrons, and they themselves organized religious, dramatic, musical, and study groups. The idea was to create an American labour force that would not resemble the wretched proletarians of England and elsewhere in Europe.

Document: Davy Crockett: A Tour of the Lowell Mills (1835)

Disenchanted with Pres. Andrew Jackson's policies on finance, land, and Native Americans, Davy Crockett, the backwoods congressman from Tennessee, turned Whig in the early 1830s. To augment the appeal of their party, the Whigs publicly displayed their new catch. As part of their display, the Whigs sponsored Crockett in a tour of the Northeast that brought him to Lowell, Mass., in 1834. The Lowell cotton mills were the showcase of American business. Although Crockett probably did not write the following narrative, which comes from An Account of Col. Crockett's Tour to the North and Down East *(1835), Lowell is accurately described.*

Next morning I rose early and started for Lowell in a fine carriage with three gentlemen who had agreed to accompany me. I had heard so much of this place that I longed to see it; not because I had heard of the "mile of gals"; no, I left that for the gallantry of the President who is admitted, on that score, to be abler than myself; but I wanted to see the power of machinery, wielded by the keenest calculations of human skill; I wanted to see how it was that these Northerners could buy cotton, and carry it home, manufacture it, bring it back, and sell it for half nothing; and in the meantime, be well to live, and make money besides.

We stopped at the large stone house at the head of the falls of the Merrimac River, and having taken a little refreshment, went down among the factories. The dinner bells were ringing, and the folks pouring out of the houses like bees out of a gum. I looked at them as they passed, all well dressed, lively, and genteel in their appearance; indeed, the girls looked as if they were coming from a quilting frolic. We took a turn round, and after dining on a fine salmon, again returned, and entered the factories.

The outdoor appearance was fully sustained by the whole of the persons employed in the different rooms. I went in among the young girls, and talked with many of them. Not one expressed herself as tired of her employment, or oppressed with work; all talked well, and looked healthy. Some of them were very handsome; and I could not help observing that they kept the prettiest inside, and put the homely ones on the outside rows....

Boott Cotton Mills, Lowell, Mass. Library of Congress, Washington, D.C.

Lowell was marveled at by foreign and domestic visitors alike but lost its idyllic character as competitive pressures within the industry resulted in larger workloads, longer hours, and smaller wages. When, in the 1840s and 1850s, Yankee young women formed embryonic unions and struck, they were replaced by French-Canadian and Irish immigrants. Nonetheless, early New England industrialism carried the imprint of a conscious sense of American exceptionalism.

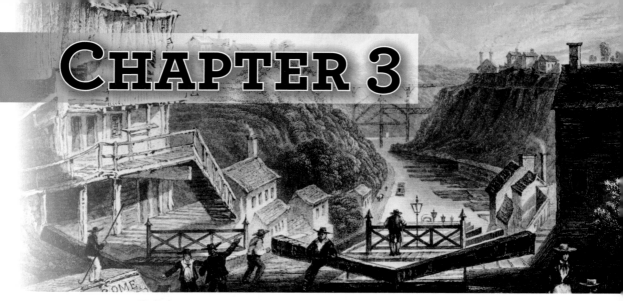

CHAPTER 3

SOCIAL DEVELOPMENTS

In the decades before the American Civil War (1861–65), the civilization of the United States exerted an irresistible pull on visitors, hundreds of whom were assigned to report back to European audiences that were fascinated by the new society and insatiable for information on every facet of the "fabled republic." What appeared to intrigue the travelers above all was the uniqueness of American society. In contrast to the relatively static and well-ordered civilization of the Old World, America seemed turbulent, dynamic, and in constant flux, its people crude but vital, awesomely ambitious, optimistic, and independent. Many well-bred Europeans were evidently taken aback by the self-assurance of lightly educated American common folk. Ordinary Americans seemed unwilling to defer to anyone on the basis of rank or status.

BIRTH OF AMERICAN CULTURE

"In the four quarters of the globe, who reads an American book?" asked an English satirist early in the 1800s. Had

Herman Melville, etching after a portrait by Joseph O. Eaton. Library of Congress, Washington, D.C. (Digital File Number: cph 3c35949)

period between 1815 and 1860 produced an outpouring of traditional literary works now known to students of English-language prose and poetry everywhere—the verse of Henry Wadsworth Longfellow and Edgar Allan Poe, the novels of James Fenimore Cooper, Nathaniel Hawthorne, and Herman Melville, as well as the essays of Ralph Waldo Emerson—all expressing distinctively American themes and depicting distinctly American characters such as Natty Bumppo, Hester Prynne, and Captain Ahab who now belong to the world.

But setting these aside, Nathaniel Bowditch's *The New American Practical Navigator* (1802), Matthew Fontaine Maury's *Physical Geography of the Sea* (1855), and the reports from the Lewis and Clark expedition and the various far Western explorations made by the U.S. Army's Corps of Engineers, as well

he looked beyond the limits of "high culture," he would have found plenty of answers. As a matter of fact, the

Document: Edgar Allan Poe: "To Science" (1829)

The ornate grotesqueries of Edgar Allan Poe's poetry and fiction often concealed the precise methods he employed to achieve his fantastic effects; similarly, his deprecation of scientific inquiry and law in "To Science" obscures the fact that Poe was knowledgeable in the science of his day and was peculiarly proud of his adeptness at "scientific reasoning." Poe intended "To Science" as both a preface and a key to his longer work, Al Aaraaf, *an allegorical tale depicting man's inadequate appreciation of God and of beauty. Poe was only 20 years old when the two poems were published in 1829 as part of his second collection,* Al Aaraaf, Tamerlane and Minor Poems.

TO SCIENCE

Science! true daughter of Old Time thou art!
Who alterest all things with thy peering eyes.

Why preyest thou thus upon the poet's heart,
Vulture, whose wings are dull realities?
How should he love thee? or how deem thee wise,
Who wouldst not leave him in his wandering
To seek for treasure in the jeweled skies,
Albeit he soared with an undaunted wing?
Hast thou not dragged Diana from her car,
And driven the Hamadryad from the wood
To seek a shelter in some happier star?
Hast thou not torn the Naiad from her flood,
The Elfin from the green grass, and from me
The summer dream beneath the tamarind tree?

Poems, New York, 1831.

as those of U.S. Navy Antarctic explorer Charles Wilkes, were the American books on the desks of sea captains, naturalists, biologists, and geologists throughout the world. By 1860 the international scientific community knew that there was an American intellectual presence.

Document: Henry Wadsworth Longfellow: "The Village Blacksmith" (1841)

Henry Wadsworth Longfellow was the best-loved poet of his time, and "The Village Blacksmith" was among his best-loved poems. The poem exhibits many of the features that recommended Longfellow to his readers: its diction is simple, its metre is regular, its moral is pleasing and easily grasped, and it is romantic and sentimental and glorifies both the American ethos and the common life. "The Village Blacksmith" was published in 1841 in the collection Ballads and Other Poems.

THE VILLAGE BLACKSMITH

Under a spreading chestnut tree
The village smithy stands;
The smith, a mighty man is he,
With large and sinewy hands;
And the muscles of his brawny arms

Are strong as iron bands.
His hair is crisp, and black, and long,
His face is like the tan;
His brow is wet with honest sweat,
He earns whate'er he can,
And looks the whole world in the face,
For he owes not any man.

Week in, week out, from morn till night,
You can hear his bellows blow;
You can hear him swing his heavy sledge
With measured beat and slow,
Like a sexton ringing the village bell,
When the evening sun is low.

And children coming home from school
Look in at the open door;
They love to see the flaming forge,
And hear the bellows roar,
And catch the burning sparks that fly
Like chaff from a threshing floor.

He goes on Sunday to the church,
And sits among his boys;
He hears the parson pray and preach,
He hears his daughter's voice
Singing in the village choir,
And it makes his heart rejoice.

It sounds to him like her mother's voice,
Singing in Paradise!
He needs must think of her once more,
How in the grave she lies;
And with his hard, rough hand he wipes
A tear out of his eyes.

Toiling — rejoicing — sorrowing,
Onward through life he goes;
Each morning sees some task begun,
Each evening sees its close;

Something attempted, something done,
Has earned a night's repose.

Thanks, thanks to thee, my worthy friend,
For the lesson thou hast taught!
Thus at the flaming forge of life
Our fortunes must be wrought;
Thus on its sounding anvil shaped
Each burning deed and thought!

Complete Poetical Works, Cambridge Edition, Boston, 1893.

At home Noah Webster's *An American Dictionary of the English Language* (1828) included hundreds of words of local origin to be incorporated in the former "King's English." Webster's blue-backed "Speller," published in 1783, the geography textbooks of Jedidiah Morse, and the *Eclectic Readers* of William Holmes McGuffey became staples in every 19th-century

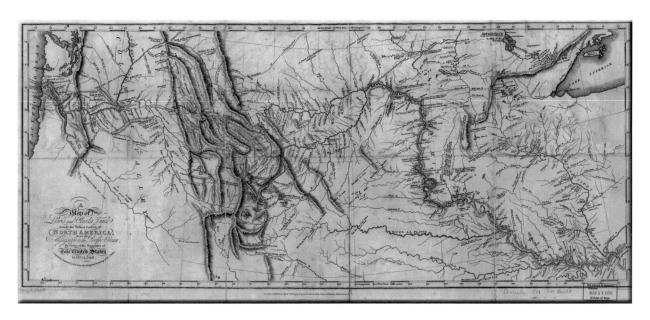

Map of William Clark and Meriwether Lewis's expedition, 1804–06. Library of Congress, Geography and Map Division, Washington, D.C.

American classroom. Popular literature included the humorous works of writers such as Seba Smith, Joseph G. Baldwin, Johnson Jones Hooper, and Artemus Ward, which featured frontier tall tales and rural dialect.

In the growing cities there were new varieties of mass entertainment,

Document: James Russell Lowell: Opposition to Nationalism in Literature (1843)

As a critic, James Russell Lowell encouraged the growth of a native literature, but he demanded that such American writing satisfy standards of literary excellence rather than national pride. In 1843 he started a monthly literary and critical journal, The Pioneer, *dedicated to the publication of good literature and criticism. The salutatory in the first issue of this short-lived endeavour (it survived only three issues) is reprinted below.*

Dr. John North, a man of some mark in his day, wrote on the first leaf of his notebook these significant words: "I beshrew his heart that gathers my opinion from anything wrote here!"

As we seated ourselves to the hard task of writing an introduction for our new literary journal, this sentence arose to our minds. It seemed to us to point clearly at the archwant of our periodical literature. We find opinions enough and to spare, but scarce any of the healthy, natural growth of our soil. If native, they are seldom more than scions of a public opinion, too often planted and watered by the prejudices or ignorant judgments of individuals, to be better than a upas tree shedding a poisonous blight on any literature that may chance to grow up under it. Or, if foreign, they are, to borrow a musical term, "recollections" of Blackwood or the quarterlies of Wilson, Macaulay, or Carlyle—not direct imitations but endeavors, as it were, to write with their cast-off pens, fresh-nibbed for cisatlantic service. The whole regiment comes one by one to our feast of letters in the same yellow domino.

Criticism, instead of being governed as it should be by the eternal and unchanging laws of beauty, which are a part of the soul's divine nature, seems rather to be a striving to reduce art to one dead level of conventional mediocrity—which only does not offend taste because it lacks even the life and strength to produce any decided impression whatever....

James Russell Lowell, photographed by Mathew Brady. Library of Congress, Washington, D.C.

P.T. Barnum's mammoth tent housing his menagerie and exhibits. Library of Congress, Washington, D.C.

including the blatantly racist minstrel shows, for which ballads like those of Stephen Foster were composed. The "museums" and circuses of P.T. Barnum also entertained the middle-class audience, and the spread of literacy sustained a new kind of popular journalism, pioneered by James Gordon Bennett, whose *New York Herald* mingled its up-to-the-moment political and international news with sports, crime, gossip, and trivia. Popular magazines such as *Harper's Weekly*, *Frank Leslie's Illustrated Newspaper*, and *Godey's Lady's Book*, edited by Sarah Josepha Hale with a keen eye toward women's wishes, also made their mark in an emerging urban America. All these added up to a flourishing democratic culture that could be dismissed as vulgar by foreign and

Document: Walt Whitman: "I Hear America Singing" (1860)

"I Hear America Singing" is one of the numerous "Inscriptions," as they were called by their author—in a modern prose work such small introductory pieces would be called epigraphs—that Walt Whitman composed, at various times, for Leaves of Grass. *This one, written in 1860, is technically beyond the time frame of this volume, as is* Leaves of Grass *itself; however, both speak directly to this moment in American culture. Whitman has been charged with the mere making of lists—of things, of persons, of ideas—and passing them off as poetry. "I Hear America Singing" is such a list, but its effectiveness is undeniable, and the notion that America is a great choral symphony made up of the individual voices of her citizens, going about their various tasks and "Singing with open mouths their strong melodious songs," is a haunting one.*

I HEAR AMERICA SINGING

I hear America singing, the varied carols I hear,
Those of mechanics, each one singing his as it should be blithe and strong,
The carpenter singing his as he measures his plank or beam,
The mason singing his as he makes ready for work, or leaves off work,
The boatman singing what belongs to him in his boat, the deck-hand singing on the steamboat deck,
The shoemaker singing as he sits on his bench, the hatter singing as he stands,
The wood-cutter's song, the ploughboy's on his way in the morning, or at noon intermission or at sundown,
The delicious singing of the mother, or of the young wife at work, or of the girl sewing or washing,
Each singing what belongs to him or her and to none else,
The day what belongs to the day—at night the party of young fellows, robust, friendly,
Singing with open mouths their strong melodious songs.

Leaves of Grass, New York, 1867.

domestic snobs but reflected a vitality loudly sung by Walt Whitman in *Leaves of Grass* (1855).

THE PEOPLE

American society was rapidly changing. Population grew at what to Europeans was an amazing rate—although it was the normal pace of American population growth for the antebellum decades—of between three-tenths and one-third per decade. After 1820 the rate of growth was not uniform throughout the country. New England and the Southern Atlantic states languished—the former region because it

Irish emigrants departing for the United States. Library of Congress, Washington, D.C.

was losing settlers to the superior farm-lands of the Western Reserve, the latter because its economy offered too few places to newcomers.

The special feature of the population increase of the 1830s and '40s was the extent to which it was composed of immigrants. Whereas about 250,000 Europeans had arrived in the first three decades of the 19th century, there were 10 times as many between 1830 and 1850. The newcomers were overwhelmingly Irish and German. Traveling in family groups rather than as individuals, they were attracted by the dazzling opportunities of American life: abundant work, land, food, and freedom on the one hand and the absence of compulsory military service on the other.

The mere statistics of immigration do not, however, tell the whole story of its vital role in pre-Civil War America. The intermingling of technology, politics, and accident produced yet another "great

Swedish immigrants en route to the western United States in the mid-19th century. Library of Congress, Washington, D.C.

migration." By the 1840s the beginnings of steam transportation on the Atlantic and improvements in the sailing speed of the last generation of windjammers made oceanic passages more frequent and regular. It became easier for hungry Europeans to answer the call of America to take up the farmlands and build the cities. Irish migration would have taken place in any case, but the catastrophe of the Irish Potato Famine of 1845–49 turned a stream into a torrent. Meanwhile, the steady growth of the democratic idea in Europe produced the Revolutions of 1848 in France, Italy, Hungary, and Germany. The uprisings in the last three countries were brutally suppressed, creating a wave of political refugees. Hence, many of the Germans who traveled over in the wake of the revolutions—the Forty-Eighters—were refugees who took liberal ideals, professional educations, and other intellectual capital to the American West. Overall German contributions to American musical, educational, and business life simply cannot be measured in statistics. Neither can one quantify the impact of the Irish politicians, policemen, and priests on American urban life or the impact of the Irish in general on Roman Catholicism in the United States.

Besides the Irish and Germans, there were thousands of Norwegians and Swedes who immigrated, driven by agricultural depression in the 1850s, to take up new land on the yet-unbroken Great Plains. And there was a much smaller migration to California in the 1850s of Chinese seeking to exchange hard times for new opportunities in the gold fields. These people, too, indelibly flavoured the culture of the United States.

Mention must also be made of utopian immigrant colonies planted by thinkers who wanted to create a new society in a New World. Examples include Nashoba, Tenn., and New Harmony, Ind., by two British newcomers, Frances Wright and Robert Dale Owen, respectively.

Document: John Humphrey Noyes: The Nashoba Community (1828)

Reformers and idealists in 19th-century America frequently felt that their aims were better served by withdrawing from society at large into semiutopian communities. One such experiment that was of short duration was the Nashoba community, founded by the social reformer Frances Wright in Tennessee in 1825. The purpose of Nashoba was to educate emancipated slaves to enable them to live in society. The following account of experiences at Nashoba is drawn from History of American Socialisms, *by John Humphrey Noyes, who was the founder of the Oneida community in New York State. The account is dated 1828, the year in which the Nashoba experiment terminated.*

This experiment was made in Shelby County, Tennessee, by the celebrated Frances Wright. The objects were to form a community in which the Negro slave should be educated and upraised to a level with the whites and thus prepared for freedom; and to set an example which, if carried out, would eventually abolish slavery in the Southern states; also to make a home for good and great men and women of all countries who might there sympathize with each other in their love and labor for humanity. She invited congenial minds from every quarter of the globe to unite with her in the search for truth and the pursuit of rational happiness. Herself a native of Scotland, she became imbued with these philanthropic views through a knowledge of the sufferings of a great portion of mankind in many countries, and of the condition of the Negro in the United States in particular.

She traveled extensively in the Southern states and explained her views to many of the planters. It was during these travels that she visited the German settlement of Rappites at Harmony, on the Wabash River, and after examining the wonderful industry of that community, she was struck with the appropriateness of their system of cooperation to the carrying out of her aspirations. She also visited some of the Shaker establishments then existing in the United States, but she thought unfavorably of them. She renewed her visits to the Rappites and was present on the occasion of their removal from Harmony to Economy on the Ohio, where she continued her acquaintance with them, receiving valuable knowledge from their experience and, as it were, witnessing a new village, with its fields, orchards, gardens, vineyards, flouring mills and manufactories, rise out of the earth beneath the hands of some 800 trained laborers....

In the autumn of 1825 [when New Harmony was under full sail in the absence of Mr. Owen], Frances Wright purchased 2,000 acres of good and pleasant woodland, lying on both sides of the Wolf River in west Tennessee, about thirteen miles above Memphis. She then purchased several Negro families, comprising fifteen able hands, and commenced her practical experiment....

There also were German planned settlements at Amana, Iowa, and in New Ulm and New Braunfels, Texas. If the growth of materialistic and expansionist bumptiousness represented by the manifest destiny movement was fueled in part by the immigration-fed expansion of the American populace, these experiments in communal living added to the less materialistic forces driving American thought. They fit the pattern of searching for heaven on earth that marked the age of reform.

Most African Americans in the North possessed theoretical freedom and little else. Confined to menial occupations for the most part, they fought a losing battle against the inroads of Irish competition in northeastern cities. The struggle between the two groups erupted spasmodically into ugly street riots. The hostility shown to free African Americans by the general community was less violent but equally unremitting. Discrimination in politics, employment, education, housing, religion, and even cemeteries resulted in a cruelly oppressive system. Unlike slaves, free African Americans in the North could criticize and petition against their subjugation, but this proved fruitless in preventing the continued deterioration of their situation.

Most Americans continued to live in the country. Although improved machinery had resulted in expanded farm production and had given further impetus to the commercialization of agriculture, the way of life of independent agriculturists had changed little by mid-century. The public journals put out by some farmers insisted that their efforts were unappreciated by the larger community. The actuality was complex. Many farmers led lives marked by unremitting toil, cash shortage, and little leisure. Farm workers received minuscule wages. In all sections of the country, much of the best land was concentrated in the hands of a small number of wealthy farmers. The proportion of farm families who owned their own land, however, was far greater in the United States than in Europe, and varied evidence points to a steady improvement in the standard and style of living of agriculturalists as mid-century approached.

CHAPTER 4

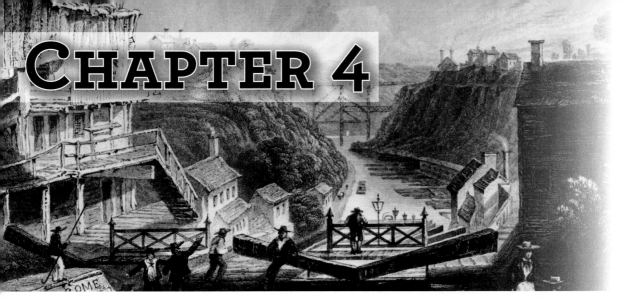

CITIES

Cities, both old and new, thrived during the era, their growth in population outstripping the spectacular growth rate of the country as a whole and their importance and influence far transcending the relatively small proportions of citizens living in them. Whether on the "urban frontier" or in the older seaboard region, antebellum cities were the centres of wealth and political influence for their outlying hinterlands. New York City, with a population approaching 500,000 by mid-century, faced problems of a different order of magnitude from those confronting such cities as Poughkeepsie, N.Y., and Newark, N.J. Yet the pattern of change during the era was amazingly similar for eastern cities or western, old cities or new, great cities or small. The lifeblood of them all was commerce. Old ideals of economy in town government were grudgingly abandoned by the merchant, professional, and landowning elites who typically ruled. Taxes were increased in order to deal with pressing new problems and to enable the urban community of mid-century to realize new opportunities. Harbours were improved, police forces professionalized, services

New York City in the 1850s. Library of Congress, Washington, D.C.

expanded, waste more reliably removed, streets improved, and welfare activities broadened, all as the result of the statesmanship and the self-interest of property owners who were convinced that amelioration was socially beneficial.

EDUCATION AND THE ROLE OF WOMEN

Cities were also centres of educational and intellectual progress. The emergence of a relatively well-financed public educational system, free of the stigma of "pauper" or "charity" schools, and the emergence of a lively "penny press," made possible by a technological revolution, were among the most important developments. The role of women in America's expanding society was intriguingly shaped by conflicting forces. On one hand, there were factors that abetted emancipation. For example, the growing cities offered new job opportunities as clerks and shop assistants for girls and young women with

Document: Catharine Beecher: The Profession of a Woman (1829)

At the beginning of the 19th century, female education had surmounted such early restrictions as that expressed in a 1684 school dictum to the effect that "all girls [shall] be excluded as improper and inconsistent with...a grammar school." Elementary education was open to all girls and secondary education to those who could afford it, but no provision had been made for higher education until Emma Willard established Troy Female Seminary (now Emma Willard School) in 1821. In 1824 Catharine Beecher, a member of an illustrious New England family, followed Mrs. Willard's lead by founding the Hartford Female Seminary. Miss Beecher explained her program for female education in the following selection from her book, Suggestions Respecting Improvements in Education, *published in 1829.*

It is to mothers and to teachers that the world is to look for the character which is to be enstamped on each succeeding generation, for it is to them that the great business of education is almost exclusively committed. And will it not appear by examination that neither mothers nor teachers have ever been properly educated for their profession? What is the *profession of a woman*? Is it not to form immortal minds, and to watch, to nurse, and to rear the bodily system, so fearfully and wonderfully made, and upon the order and regulation of which the health and well-being of the mind so greatly depends?

But let most of our sex, upon whom these arduous duties devolve, be asked: Have you ever devoted any time and study, in the course of your education, to any preparation for these duties? Have you been taught anything of the structure, the nature, and the laws of the body which you inhabit? Were you ever taught to understand the operation of diet, air, exercise, and modes of dress upon the human frame? Have the causes which are continually operating to prevent good health and the modes by which it might be perfected and preserved ever been made the subject of any *instruction*? Perhaps almost every voice would respond, no. We have attended to almost everything more than to this; we have been taught more concerning the structure of the earth, the laws of the heavenly bodies, the habits and formation of plants, the philosophy of languages—more of *almost anything* than the structure of the human frame and the laws of health and reason....

elementary educations furnished by the public schools.

And the need for trained teachers for those schools offered another avenue to female independence. At higher levels, new rungs on the ladder of upward mobility were provided by the creation of women's colleges, such as Mount Holyoke in South Hadley, Mass. (1837), and by the admission of women to a very few coeducational colleges, such as Oberlin (1833) and Antioch (1852), both in Ohio. A rare woman or two even broke into professional ranks, including Elizabeth Blackwell, considered the first woman physician of modern times, and the Rev. Olympia Brown, one of the first American women whose ordination was sanctioned by a full denomination.

On the other hand, traditionally educated women from genteel families remained bound by silken cords of expectation. The "duties of womanhood" expounded by popular media included, to the exclusion of all else, the conservation of a husband's resources, the religious and moral education of children and servants, and the cultivation of higher sensibilities through the proper selection of decorative objects and reading matter. The "true woman" made the home an island of tranquility and uplift to which the busy male could retreat after a day's struggle in the hard

Elizabeth Blackwell. Museum of the City of New York/Archive Photos/Getty Images

world of the marketplace. In so doing, she was venerated but kept in a clearly noncompetitive role.

Elizabeth Blackwell

Elizabeth Blackwell was of a large, prosperous, and cultured English family and was well educated by private tutors. Financial reverses and the family's liberal social and religious views prompted them to immigrate to the United States in the summer of 1832. Soon after taking up residence in New York, her father, Samuel Blackwell, became active in abolitionist activities. The Blackwells moved to Jersey City, N.J., in 1835 and to Cincinnati, Ohio, in 1838. Soon afterward Samuel Blackwell's death left the family in poverty, and Elizabeth and two sisters opened a private school. Later Elizabeth taught school in Henderson, Ky., and in 1845–47 in North and South Carolina.

During the latter period Elizabeth Blackwell undertook the study of medicine privately with sympathetic physicians, and in 1847 she began seeking admission to a medical school. All the leading schools rejected her application, but she was at length admitted, almost by fluke, to Geneva Medical College (a forerunner of Hobart College) in Geneva, N.Y. Her months there were extremely difficult. Townspeople and much of the male student body ostracized and harassed her, and she was at first even barred from classroom demonstration. She persevered, however, and in January 1849, ranked first in her class, she became the first woman in the United States to graduate from medical school and the first modern-day woman doctor of medicine.

In April, having become a naturalized U.S. citizen, Blackwell traveled to England to seek further training, and in May she went on to Paris, where in June she entered the midwives' course at La Maternité. While there she contracted an infectious eye disease that left her blind in one eye and forced her to abandon hope of becoming a surgeon. In October 1850 she returned to England and worked at St. Bartholomew's Hospital under Dr. (later Sir) James Paget. In the summer of 1851 she returned to New York, where she was refused posts in the city's hospitals and dispensaries and was even unable to rent private consulting quarters. Her private practice was very slow to develop, and in the meantime she wrote a series of lectures, published in 1852 as *The Laws of Life, with Special Reference to the Physical Education of Girls*.

In 1853 Blackwell opened a small dispensary in a slum district. Within a few years she was joined by her younger sister, Dr. Emily Blackwell, and by Dr. Marie E. Zakrzewska, and in May 1857 the dispensary, greatly enlarged, was incorporated as the New York Infirmary for Women and Children. In January 1859, during a year-long lecture tour of Great Britain, she became the first woman to have her name placed on the British medical register. At the outbreak of the American Civil War in 1861, she helped organize the Woman's Central Association of Relief and the U.S. Sanitary Commission and worked mainly through the former to select and train nurses for war service.

In November 1868 a plan long in the perfecting, developed in large part in consultation with Florence Nightingale in England, bore fruit in the opening of the Woman's Medical College at the infirmary. Elizabeth Blackwell set very high standards for admission, academic and clinical training, and certification for the school, which continued in operation for 31 years; she herself occupied the chair of hygiene. In 1869 Blackwell moved permanently to England. She established a successful private practice, helped organize the National Health Society in 1871, and in 1875 was appointed professor of gynecology at the London School of Medicine for Women. She retained the latter position until 1907, when an injury forced her to retire. Among her other writings are *The Religion of Health* (1871), *Counsel to Parents on the Moral Education of Their Children* (1878), *The Human Element in Sex* (1884), her autobiographical *Pioneer Work in Opening the Medical Profession to Women* (1895), and *Essays in Medical Sociology* (1902).

WEALTH

The brilliant French visitor Alexis de Tocqueville, in common with most contemporary observers, believed American society to be remarkably egalitarian. Most rich American men were thought to have been born poor; "self-made" was the term Henry Clay popularized for them. The society was allegedly a very fluid one, marked by the rapid rise and fall of fortunes, with room at the top accessible to all but the most humble; opportunity for success seemed freely available to all, and, although material possessions were not distributed perfectly equally, they were, in theory, dispersed so fairly that only a few poor and a few rich men existed at either end of the social spectrum.

The actuality, however, was far different. While the rich were inevitably not numerous, America by 1850 had more millionaires than all of Europe. New York, Boston, and Philadelphia each had perhaps 1,000 individuals admitting to assets of $100,000 or more, at a time when wealthy taxpayers kept secret from assessors the bulk of their wealth. Because an annual income of $4,000 or $5,000 enabled a person to live luxuriously, these were great fortunes indeed. Typically, the wealthiest 1 percent of urban citizens owned approximately one-half the wealth of

Cornelius Vanderbilt, a shipping and railroad magnate, was a millionaire by 1846, and acquired over $100,000,000 in his personal fortune over the course of his life. Library of Congress Prints and Photographs Division

the great cities of the Northeast, while the great bulk of their populations possessed little or nothing.

Document: Thomas Skidmore: The Unequal Distribution of Property (1829)

The Jacksonian Era was marked by two major reform movements: one, that of the New England humanitarians, religious and philosophical in nature; the other, organized among workingmen, secular and practical. Thomas Skidmore, a leader of the short-lived New York Workingmen's Party, was deeply concerned with the plight of workers who he thought were oppressed by the industrial and banking interests. Skidmore's major reform treatise, The Rights of Man to Property!, *analyzed the exploitation of workers and set forth a program for the periodic redistribution of property and the abolition of monopolies and inherited wealth. Portions of the book's concluding chapter are presented here.*

If a man were to ask me to what I would compare the unequal distribution of property which prevails in the world, and has ever prevailed, I would say that it reminds me of a large party of gentlemen who should have a common right to dine at one and the same public table; a part of whom should arrive first, sit down and eat what they chose, and, then, because the remaining part came later to dinner, should undertake to monopolize the whole and deprive them of the opportunity of satisfying their hunger, but upon terms such as those who had feasted should be pleased to prescribe.

Such, now, is the actual condition of the whole human race. Those who have gone before us have been the first to sit down to the table and to enjoy themselves without interruption from those who came afterward; and, not content with this enjoyment, they have disposed of the whole dinner in such a manner that nine-tenths of the beings that now people this globe have not wherewith to dine, but upon terms such as these first monopolizers, or those to whom they pretend they have conferred their own power as successors, shall choose to dictate. It is as if, after dining till they were satisfied, a general scramble ensued for what remained on the table; and those who succeeded in filling their pockets and other receptacles with provisions should have something to give to their children; but those who should have the misfortune to get none, or having got it, should lose it again, through fraud, calamity, or force, should have none for theirs, to the latest generation....

In what has long been called the "Age of the Common Man," rich men were almost invariably born not into humble or poor families but into wealthy and prestigious ones. In western cities, too, class lines increasingly hardened after 1830. The common man lived in the age, but he did not dominate it. It appears that contemporaries, overimpressed with the absence of a titled aristocracy and with the democratic tone and manner of American life, failed to see the extent to which money, family, and status exerted power in the New World even as they did in the Old.

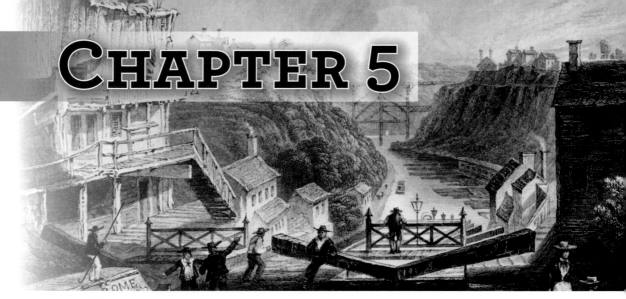

CHAPTER 5

JACKSONIAN DEMOCRACY

The election of 1828 is commonly regarded as a turning point in the political history of the United States. Andrew Jackson was the first president from the area west of the Appalachians, but it was equally significant that the initiative in launching his candidacy and much of the leadership in the organization of his campaign also came from the West. The victory of Jackson indicated a westward movement of the centre of political power. He was also the first man to be elected president through a direct appeal to the mass of the voters rather than through the support of a recognized political organization. Jackson once said: "I know what I am fit for. I can command a body of men in a rough way; but I am not fit to be president." Yet today he is regarded as the maker of the modern presidency.

THE DEMOCRATIZATION OF POLITICS

American politics became increasingly democratic during the 1820s and '30s. Local and state offices that had earlier been appointive became elective. Suffrage was expanded as property and other restrictions on voting were reduced or abandoned in most states. The freehold requirement that had

Serving as a major general during the War of 1812, Andrew Jackson was hailed as a military hero for his successes in battle and gained widespread popularity in the West—a factor that fueled his eventual election to the presidency in 1828. Stock Montage/Archive Photos/Getty Images denied voting to all but holders of real estate was almost everywhere discarded before 1820, while the taxpaying qualification was also removed, if more slowly and gradually. In many states a printed ballot replaced the earlier system of voice voting, while the secret ballot also grew in favour. Whereas in 1800 only two states provided for the popular choice of presidential electors, by 1832 only South Carolina still left the decision to the legislature. Conventions of elected delegates increasingly replaced legislative or congressional caucuses as the agencies for making party nominations. By the latter change, a system for nominating candidates by self-appointed cliques meeting in secret was replaced by a system of open selection of candidates by democratically elected bodies.

Document: A Plea for Manhood Suffrage (1829)

A significant characteristic of the Jacksonian Era was the movement to expand the base of popular power by extending the right to vote to those who did not own property. The Virginia Convention of 1829, called to revise the state's constitution of 1776, was divided on the question. Former president James Monroe and former senator John Randolph, both delegates at the convention, were opposed to any extension of suffrage, fearing that it would erode the rights of property. Others argued that failure to liberalize the constitution would betray fundamental American principles. The following Memorial of the Non-Freeholders of Richmond, Va., urging expanded suffrage, was presented to the convention by John Marshall, chief justice of the Supreme Court. In the end, James Madison negotiated a compromise by which general manhood suffrage was rejected, but property qualifications for voting were relaxed.

Your memorialists, as their designation imports, belong to that class of citizens who, not having the good fortune to possess a certain portion of land, are, for that cause only, debarred from the enjoyment of the right of suffrage....

Comprising a very large part, probably a majority, of male citizens of mature age, they have been passed by, like aliens or slaves, as if destitute of interest, or unworthy of a voice, in measures involving their future political destiny; while the free-holders, sole possessors, under the existing Constitution, of the elective franchise have, upon the strength of that possession alone, asserted and maintained in themselves the exclusive power of new-modeling the fundamental laws of the state: in other words, have seized upon the sovereign authority....

Among the doctrines inculcated in the great charter handed down to us as a declaration of the rights pertaining to the good people of Virginia and their posterity, "as the basis and foundation of government," we are taught,

> **That all men are by nature equally free and independent, and have certain inherent rights, of which, when they enter into a state of society, they cannot, by any compact, deprive or divest their posterity: namely, the enjoyment of life and liberty, with the means of acquiring and possessing property, and pursuing and obtaining happiness and safety....**

These democratic changes were not engineered by Andrew Jackson and his followers, as was once believed. Most of them antedated the emergence of Jackson's Democratic Party, and in New York, Mississippi, and other states some of the reforms were accomplished over the objections of the Jacksonians. There were men in all sections who feared the spread of political democracy, but by the 1830s few were willing to voice such misgivings publicly. Jacksonians effectively sought to fix the impression that they alone were champions of democracy, engaged in mortal struggle against aristocratic opponents. The accuracy of such propaganda varied according to local circumstances. The great political reforms of the early 19th century in actuality were conceived by no one faction or party. The real question about these reforms concerns the extent to which they truly represented the victory of democracy in the United States.

Small cliques or entrenched "machines" dominated democratically elected nominating conventions as earlier they had controlled caucuses. While by the 1830s the common man—of European descent—had come into possession of the vote in most states, the nomination process continued to be outside his control. More important, the policies adopted by competing factions and parties in the states owed little to ordinary voters. The legislative programs of the "regencies" and juntos that effectively ran state politics were designed primarily to reward the party faithful and to keep them in power. State parties extolled the common people in grandiloquent terms but characteristically focused on prosaic legislation that awarded bank charters or monopoly rights to construct transportation projects to favoured insiders. That American parties would be pragmatic vote-getting coalitions, rather than organizations devoted to high political principles, was due largely to another series of reforms enacted during the era. Electoral changes that rewarded winners or plurality gatherers in small districts, in contrast to a previous system that divided a state's offices among the several leading vote getters, worked against the chances of "single issue" or "ideological" parties while strengthening parties that tried to be many things to many people.

THE JACKSONIANS

To his army of followers, Jackson was the embodiment of popular democracy. A truly self-made man of strong will and courage, he personified for many citizens the vast power of nature and Providence, on the one hand, and the majesty of the people, on the other. His very weaknesses, such as a nearly uncontrollable temper, were political strengths. Opponents who branded him an enemy of property and order only gave credence to the claim of Jackson's supporters that he stood for the poor against the rich, the plain people against the interests.

Jackson, like most of his leading antagonists, was in fact a wealthy man of conservative social beliefs. In his

Document: Mrs. Samuel Harrison Smith: The Inauguration of Andrew Jackson (1829)

The successor to a long line of "patrician" presidents, Andrew Jackson was widely acclaimed as the "peoples' choice" and the symbol of the new "age of the common man." Jackson brought with him to the White House a reputation as a military hero and an image as a frontiersman. He had the support of Western farmers and Eastern workingmen, who flocked to Washington to celebrate his inauguration. Mrs. Samuel Harrison Smith, grande dame of Washington society, set down the following horrified eyewitness account of that tumultuous day in March 1829 in a letter to a friend written a few days after the event.

It [the inauguration]...was not a thing of detail or a succession of small incidents. No, it was one grand whole, an imposing and majestic spectacle, and, to a reflective mind, one of moral sublimity. Thousands and thousands of people, without distinction of rank, collected in an immense mass round the Capitol, silent, orderly, and tranquil, with their eyes fixed on the front of that edifice, waiting the appearance of the President in the portico. The door from the rotunda opens; preceded by the marshals, surrounded by the judges of the Supreme Court, the old man with his gray locks, that crown of glory, advances, bows to the people who greet him with a shout that rends the air. The cannons from the heights around, from Alexandria and Fort Warburton, proclaim the oath he has taken and all the hills reverberate the sound. It was grand; it was sublime! An almost breathless silence succeeded, and the multitude was still, listening to catch the sound of his voice, though it was so low as to be heard only by those nearest to him.

After reading his speech; the oath was administered to him by the chief justice. Then Marshall presented the Bible. The President took it from his hands, pressed his lips to it, laid it reverently down, then bowed again to the people — yes, to the people in all their majesty. And had the spectacle closed here, even Europeans must have acknowledged that a free people, collected in their might, silent, and tranquil, restrained solely by a moral power, without a shadow around of military force, was majesty rising to sublimity and far surpassing the majesty of kings and princes surrounded with armies and glittering in gold....

many volumes of correspondence he rarely referred to labour. As a lawyer and man of affairs in Tennessee prior to his accession to the presidency, he aligned himself not with have-nots but with the influential, not with the debtor but with the creditor. His reputation was created largely by astute men who propagated the belief that his party was the people's party and that the policies of his administrations were in the popular interest. Savage attacks on those policies by some wealthy critics only fortified the belief that the Jacksonian movement was radical as well as democratic.

At its birth in the mid-1820s, the Jacksonian, or Democratic, Party was a loose coalition of diverse men and interests united primarily by a practical vision. They held to the twin beliefs that Old Hickory, as Jackson was known, was a magnificent candidate and that his election to the presidency would benefit those who helped bring it about. His excellence as candidate derived in part from the fact that he appeared to have no known political principles of any sort. In this period there were no distinct parties on the national level. Jackson, Clay, John C. Calhoun, John Quincy Adams, and William H. Crawford—the leading presidential aspirants—all portrayed themselves as "Republicans," followers of the party of the revered Jefferson. The National Republicans were the followers of Adams and Clay; the Whigs, who emerged in 1834, were, above all else, the party dedicated to the defeat of Jackson.

THE MAJOR PARTIES

The great parties of the era were thus created to attain victory for men rather than measures. Once the parties were in being, their leaders understandably sought to convince the electorate of the primacy of principles. It is noteworthy, however, that former Federalists at first flocked to the new parties in largely equal numbers and that men on opposite sides of such issues

Collectively known as the Great Triumverate, Daniel Webster (left), Henry Clay (centre), and John C. Calhoun were renowned statesmen united in opposition to many of Jackson's policies and variously affiliated with the Whig Party. Kean Collection/Archive Photos/Getty Images

as internal improvements or a national bank could unite behind Jackson. With the passage of time, the parties did come increasingly to be identified with distinctive, and opposing, political policies.

By the 1840s, Whig and Democratic congressmen voted as rival blocs. Whigs supported and Democrats opposed a weak executive, a new Bank of the United States, a high tariff, distribution of land revenues to the states, relief legislation to mitigate the effects of the depression, and federal reapportionment of House seats. Whigs voted against and Democrats approved an independent treasury, an aggressive foreign policy, and expansionism. These were important issues, capable of dividing the electorate just as they divided the major parties in Congress. Certainly it was significant that Jacksonians were more ready than their opponents to take punitive measures against African Americans or abolitionists or to banish and use other forceful measures against the southern Indian tribes, brushing aside treaties protecting Native American rights. But these differences do not substantiate the belief that the Democrats and Whigs were divided ideologically, with only the former somehow representing the interests of the propertyless.

Party lines earlier had been more easily broken, as during the crisis that erupted over South Carolina's bitter objections to the high Tariff of 1828. Jackson's firm opposition to Calhoun's policy of nullification (i.e., the right of a state to nullify a federal law, in this case the tariff) had commanded wide support within and outside the Democratic Party. Clay's solution to the crisis, a compromise tariff, represented not an ideological split with Jackson but Clay's ability to conciliate and to draw political advantage from astute tactical maneuvering.

Document: John C. Calhoun: States' Rights and Nullification (1832)

When South Carolina responded to the Tariff of 1832 by asserting the doctrine of nullification, John C. Calhoun resigned the vice presidency to speak for his state in the Senate. He wrote the following Address to the People of the United States *to accompany the Ordinance of Nullification of Nov. 24, 1832. In the address, based upon the "South Carolina Exposition" he had written secretly four years earlier, Calhoun set forth South Carolina's objections to the protective tariff and his state rights theory of the Constitution. The latter has enjoyed lasting popularity with groups intent on defending minority and sectional interests.*

We, the people of South Carolina, assembled in convention in our sovereign capacity as one of the parties to the compact which formed the Constitution of the United States, have declared the act of Congress, approved the 14th of July, 1832, to alter and amend the several acts imposing duties on imports, and the acts which it alters and amends to be unconstitutional, and therefore null and void; and have invested the legislature of the state with power to adopt such measures, not repugnant to the Constitution of the United States nor of this state, as it may deem proper to carry the same into effect. In taking this step, we feel it to be due to the intimate political relations existing between the states of the Union, to make known to them, distinctly, the principles on which we have acted, with the cause and motive by which we have been influenced, to fulfill which is the object of the present communication.

For this purpose, it will be necessary to state, summarily, what we conceive to be the nature and character of the Constitution of the United States, with the rights and duties of the states — so far as they relate to the subject — in reference both to the Union and to their own citizens; and also the character and effect, in a political point of view, of the system of protective duties contained in the acts which we have declared to be unconstitutional, as far as it may be necessary, in reference to the same subject....

The Jacksonians depicted their war on the second Bank of the United States as a struggle against an alleged aristocratic monster that oppressed the West, debtor farmers, and poor people generally. Jackson's decisive reelection in 1832 was once interpreted as a sign of popular agreement with the Democratic

The building that once housed the Second Bank of the United States still stands in Philadelphia. Shutterstock.com

interpretation of the Bank War, but more recent evidence discloses that Jackson's margin was hardly unprecedented and that Democratic success may have been due to other considerations. The second Bank was evidently well thought of by many Westerners, many farmers, and even Democratic politicians who admitted to opposing it primarily not to incur the wrath of Jackson.

Jackson's reasons for detesting the second Bank and its president (Nicholas Biddle) were complex. Anticapitalist ideology would not explain a Jacksonian policy that replaced a quasi-national bank as repository of government funds with dozens of state and private banks, equally controlled by capitalists and even more dedicated than was Biddle to profit making. The saving virtue of these "pet banks" appeared to be the Democratic political affiliations of their directors. Perhaps the pragmatism as well as the large degree of similarity between the Democrats and

Whigs is best indicated by their frank adoption of the "spoils system." The Whigs, while out of office, denounced the vile Democratic policy for turning lucrative customhouse and other posts over to supporters, but once in office they resorted to similar practices. It is of interest that the Jacksonian appointees were hardly more plebeian than were their so-called aristocratic predecessors.

MINOR PARTIES

The politics of principle was represented during the era not by the major parties but by the minor ones. The Anti-Masons aimed to stamp out an alleged aristocratic conspiracy. The Workingmen's Party called for "social justice." The Locofocos (so named after the matches they used to light up their first meeting in a hall darkened by their opponents) denounced monopolists in the Democratic Party and out.

Locofoco Party

Made up primarily of workingmen and reformers, the Locofoco Party was a radical wing of the Democratic Party that organized in New York City in 1835. It was opposed to state banks, monopolies, paper money, tariffs, and generally any financial policies that seemed to its members to be antidemocratic and conducive to special privilege. The Locofocos received their name (which was later derisively applied by political opponents to all Democrats) when party regulars in New York turned off the gas lights to oust the radicals from a Tammany Hall nominating meeting. The radicals responded by lighting candles with the new self-igniting friction matches known as locofocos, and proceeded to nominate their own slate.

Never a national party, the Locofocos reached their peak when Pres. Martin Van Buren urged and Congress passed (July 4, 1840) the Independent Treasury Act; it fulfilled the primary Locofoco aim: complete separation of government from banking. After 1840 Locofoco political influence was largely confined to New York, and by the end of the decade many Locofocos were allied with the Barnburner Democrats, who eventually left the party over the slavery extension issue.

The variously named nativist parties accused the Roman Catholic Church of all manner of evil. The Liberty Party opposed the spread of slavery. All these parties were ephemeral because they proved incapable of mounting a broad appeal that attracted masses of voters in addition to their original constituencies. The Democratic and Whig parties thrived not in spite of their opportunism but because of it, reflecting well the practical spirit that animated most American voters.

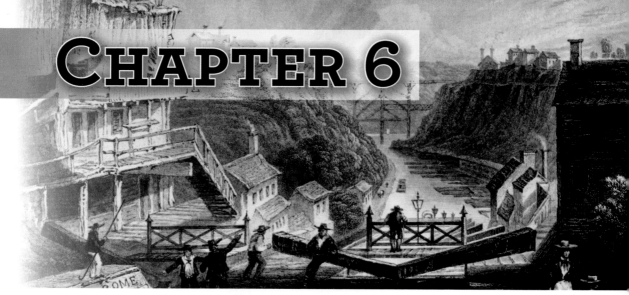

CHAPTER 6

AN AGE OF REFORM

Historians have labeled the period 1830–50 an "age of reform." At the same time that the pursuit of the dollar was becoming so frenzied that some observers called it the country's true religion, tens of thousands of Americans joined an array of movements dedicated to spiritual and secular uplift. There is not yet agreement as to why a rage for reform erupted in the antebellum decades. A few of the explanations cited, none of them conclusive, include an outburst of Protestant Evangelicalism, a reform spirit that swept across the Anglo-American community, a delayed reaction to the perfectionist teachings of the Enlightenment, and the worldwide revolution in communications that was a feature of 19th-century capitalism.

What is not in question is the amazing variety of reform movements that flourished simultaneously in the North—women's rights, pacifism, temperance, prison reform, abolition of imprisonment for debt, an end to capital punishment, improving the conditions of the working classes, a system of universal education, the organization of communities that discarded private property, improving the condition of the insane and the congenitally enfeebled, and the regeneration

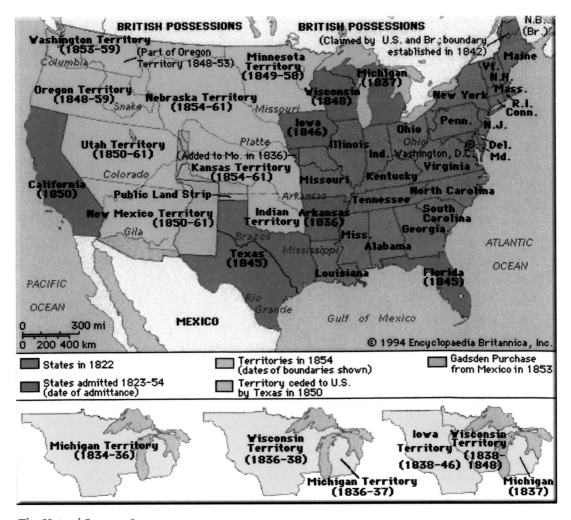

The United States, 1822–54.

of the individual were among the causes that inspired zealots during the era.

The strangest thing about American life was its combination of economic hunger and spiritual striving. Both rested on the conviction that the future could be controlled and improved. Life might have been cruel and harsh on the frontier, but there was a strong belief that the human condition was sure to change for the better: human nature itself was not stuck in the groove of perpetual shortcoming, as old-time Calvinism had predicted.

The period of "freedom's ferment" from 1830 to 1860 combined the humanitarian impulses of the late 18th century with the revivalistic pulse of the early 19th century. The two streams flowed together. For example, the earnest Christians who founded the American Christian Missionary Society believed it to be their duty to bring the good news of salvation through Jesus Christ to the "heathens" of Asia. But in carrying out this imperious assault on the religions of the poor in China and India, they founded schools and hospitals that greatly improved the earthly lot of their Chinese and "Hindoo" converts in a manner of which Jefferson might have approved.

Millennialism—the belief that the world might soon end and had to be purged of sin before Christ's Second Coming (as preached by revivalists such as Charles Grandison Finney)—found its counterpart in secular perfectionism, which held that it was possible to abolish every form of social and personal suffering through achievable changes in the way the world worked. Hence, a broad variety of crusades and crusaders flourished. Universal education was seen as the key to it all, which accounted for many college foundings and for the push toward universal free public schooling led by Horace Mann, who went from being the secretary to Massachusetts's State Board of Education to being the president of Antioch College, where he told his students to "be ashamed to die until you have won some victory for humanity."

One way to forge such victories was to improve the condition of those whom fate had smitten and society had

Reverend Charles G. Finney, 1835 engraving. Library of Congress, Washington, D.C.

neglected or abused. There was, for example, the movement to provide special education for the deaf, led by Samuel Gridley Howe, as well as the founding of an institute to teach the blind by Boston merchant Thomas Handasyd Perkins, who found philanthropy a good way for a Christian businessman to show his appreciation for what he saw as God's blessings on his enterprises. There also was the work of Dorothea Lynde Dix to humanize the appalling treatment of the insane, which followed up on the precedent set by Benjamin Rush, signer of the Declaration of Independence, a devout believer in God and science.

Charles Fourier. Library of Congress, Washington, D.C.

As the march of industrialization made thousands of workers dependent on the uncontrollable ups and downs of the business cycle and the generosity of employers—described by some at the time as "putting the living of the many in the hands of the few"—the widening imbalance between classes spurred economic reformers to action. Some accepted the permanence of capitalism but tried to enhance the bargaining power of employees through labour unions. Others rejected the private enterprise model and looked to a reorganization of society on cooperative rather than competitive lines. Such was the basis of Fourierism (the philosophy of social reform developed by French social theorist Charles Fourier)

and utopian socialism. One labour reformer, George Henry Evans, proposed that wages be raised by reducing the supply of labourers through awarding some of them free farms, "homesteads" carved from the public domain. Even some of the fighters for immigration restriction who belonged to what was known as the Know-Nothing Party had the same aim—namely, to preserve jobs for the native-born. Other reformers focused on peripheral issues such as the healthier diet expounded by Sylvester Graham or the sensible women's dress advocated by Amelia Jenks Bloomer, both of whom saw these small steps as leading toward more rational and gentle human behaviour overall.

Whatever a reform movement's nature, whether as pragmatic as agricultural improvement or as utopian as universal peace, the techniques that spread the message over America's broad expanses were similar. Voluntary associations were formed to spread the word and win supporters, a practice that Tocqueville, in 1841, found to be a key to American democracy. Even when church-affiliated, these groups were usually directed by professional men rather than ministers, and lawyers were conspicuously numerous. Next came publicity through organizational newspapers, which were easy to found on small amounts of capital and sweat. So when, as one observer noted, almost every American had a plan for the universal improvement of society in his pocket, every other American was likely to be aware of it.

Document: The Seneca Falls Declaration on Women's Rights (1848)

The organized movement for equal rights for women got formally under way with the Seneca Falls (N.Y.) Convention, called by two female abolitionists, Lucretia Mott and Elizabeth Cady Stanton, and held on July 19 and 20, 1848. A Declaration of Sentiments (an excerpt of which begins below) and 12 resolutions (also excerpted) were adopted at the meeting. The 11th resolution may not have been adopted by the full convention. At a second convention in August, the movement took organizational shape and thereafter spread quickly throughout the North and Northwest.

When, in the course of human events, it becomes necessary for one portion of the family of man to assume among the people of the earth a position different from that which they have hitherto occupied, but one to which the laws of nature and of nature's God entitle them, a decent respect to the opinions of mankind requires that they should declare the causes that impel them to such a course.

We hold these truths to be self-evident: that all men and women are created equal; that they are endowed by their Creator with certain inalienable rights; that among these are life, liberty, and the pursuit of happiness; that to secure these rights governments are instituted, deriving their just powers from the consent of the governed. Whenever any form of government becomes destructive of these ends, it is the right of those who suffer from it to refuse allegiance to it, and to insist upon the institution of a new government, laying its foundation on such principles, and organizing its powers in such form, as to them shall seem most likely to effect their safety and happiness.

Prudence, indeed, will dictate that governments long established should not be changed for light and transient causes; and, accordingly, all experience has shown that mankind are more disposed to suffer, while evils are sufferable, than to right themselves by abolishing the forms to which they were accustomed. But when a long train of abuses and usurpations, pursuing invariably the same object, evinces a design to reduce them under absolute despotism, it is their duty to throw off such government and to provide new guards for their future security. Such has been the patient sufferance of the women under this government, and such is now the necessity which constrains them to demand the equal station to which they are entitled....

Two of these crusades lingered in strength well beyond the Civil War era. Temperance was one, probably because it invoked lasting values—moralism, efficiency, and health. Drinking was viewed as a sin that, if overindulged, led to alcoholism, incurred social costs, hurt productivity, and harmed one's body. The women's rights crusade, which first came to national attention in the Seneca Falls Convention of 1848, persisted because it touched upon a perennial and universal question of the just allotment of gender roles.

ABOLITIONISM

Finally and fatally there was abolitionism, the antislavery movement. Passionately advocated and resisted with equal intensity, it appeared as late as the 1850s to be a failure in politics. Yet by 1865 it had succeeded in embedding its goal in the Constitution by amendment, though at the cost of a civil war. At its core lay the issue of "race," over which Americans have shown their best and worst faces for more than three centuries. When it became entangled in this period with the dynamics of American sectional conflict, its full explosive potential was released.

William Lloyd Garrison. Library of Congress, Washington, D.C.

If the reform impulse was a common one uniting the American people in the mid-19th century, its manifestation in abolitionism finally split them apart for four bloody years.

Abolition itself was a diverse phenomenon. At one end of its spectrum was William Lloyd Garrison, an "immediatist," who denounced not only slavery but the Constitution of the United States for tolerating the evil. His newspaper, *The Liberator*, lived up to its promise that it would not equivocate in its war against slavery. Garrison's uncompromising tone infuriated not only the South but many Northerners as well and was long treated as though it were typical of abolitionism in general. Actually it was not. At the other end of the abolitionist spectrum and in between stood such men and women as Theodore Weld, James Gillespie Birney, Gerrit Smith, Theodore Parker, Julia Ward Howe, Lewis Tappan, Salmon P. Chase, and Lydia Maria Child, all of whom represented a variety of stances, all more conciliatory than Garrison's. James Russell Lowell, whose emotional balance was cited by a biographer as proof that abolitionists need not have been unstable, urged in contrast to Garrison that "the world must be healed by degrees." Also of importance was the work of free blacks such as David Walker and Robert Forten and ex-slaves such as Frederick Douglass, who had the clearest of all reasons to work for the cause but who shared some broader

Lydia M. Child at age 22. Library of Congress, Washington, D.C.

humanitarian motives with their white coworkers.

Whether they were Garrisonians or not, abolitionist leaders have been scorned as cranks who were either working out their own personal maladjustments or as people using the slavery issue to restore a status that as an alleged New England elite they feared they were losing. The truth may be simpler. Few neurotics and few members of the northern socioeconomic elite became abolitionists. For all the movement's zeal and propagandistic successes, it was bitterly resented by many Northerners, and the masses of free whites were indifferent to its message. In the 1830s urban mobs, typically led by "gentlemen of property and standing," stormed abolitionist meetings, wreaking violence on the property and persons of African Americans and their white sympathizers, evidently indifferent to the niceties distinguishing one abolitionist theorist from another. The fact that abolition leaders were remarkably similar in their New England backgrounds, their Calvinist self-righteousness, their high social status, and the relative excellence of their educations is hardly evidence that

Document: William Lloyd Garrison: For Immediate Abolition (1831)

Sometime during the year 1829, William Lloyd Garrison changed his mind about African American slavery. He had always advocated its abolition, but he had been a gradualist, holding that a slow, steady movement in the direction of freedom would be better for whites and African Americans alike. But now he rejected this position, which he came to condemn, for "has not the experience of two centuries," he would say with his new understanding, "shown that gradualism in theory is perpetuity in practice?" The change of heart would not be important if it had not, for all practical purposes, launched the movement known as militant Abolitionism. Probably the most influential organ of this movement was The Liberator, *which Garrison edited from its first issue, in January 1831, to its last, in December 1865—the month that saw the ratification of the*

Thirteenth Amendment, outlawing slavery. Portions of the famous salutatory of The Liberator's *first issue are reprinted below.*

In the month of August I issued proposals for publishing the *Liberator* in Washington City; but the enterprise, though hailed in different sections of the country, was palsied by public indifference. Since that time, the removal of the *Genius of Universal Emancipation* to the seat of government has rendered less imperious the establishment of a similar periodical in that quarter.

During my recent tour for the purpose of exciting the minds of the people by a series of discourses on the subject of slavery, every place that I visited gave fresh evidence of the fact that a greater revolution in public sentiment was to be effected in the free states — *and particularly in New England* — than at the South. I found contempt more bitter, opposition more active, detraction more relentless, prejudice more stubborn, and apathy more frozen than among slaveowners themselves. Of course, there were individual exceptions to the contrary. This state of things afflicted but did not dishearten me. I determined, at every hazard, to lift up the standard of emancipation in the eyes of the nation, *within sight of Bunker Hill and in the birthplace of liberty.* That standard is now unfurled; and long may it float, unhurt by the spoliations of time or the missiles of a desperate foe — yea, till every chain be broken and every bondman set free! Let Southern oppressors tremble; let their secret abettors tremble; let their Northern apologists tremble; let all the enemies of the persecuted blacks tremble.

I deem the publication of my original prospectus unnecessary, as it has obtained a wide circulation. The principles therein inculcated will be steadily pursued in this paper, excepting that I shall not array myself as the political partisan of any man. In defending the great cause of human rights, I wish to derive the assistance of all religions and of all parties....

their cause was either snobbish or elitist. Ordinary citizens were more inclined to loathe African Americans and to preoccupy themselves with personal advance within the system.

SUPPORT OF REFORM MOVEMENTS

The existence of many reform movements did not mean that a vast number of Americans supported them. Abolition did poorly at the polls. Some reforms were more popular than others, but by and large none of the major movements had mass followings. The evidence indicates that few persons actually participated in these activities. Utopian communities such as Brook Farm and those in New Harmony, Ind., and Oneida, N.Y., did not succeed in winning over many followers or in inspiring many other groups to imitate their example. The importance of these and the other movements derived neither from their size nor from their achievements. Reform reflected the sensitivity of a small number of persons to imperfections in American life. In a sense, the reformers were "voices of conscience,"

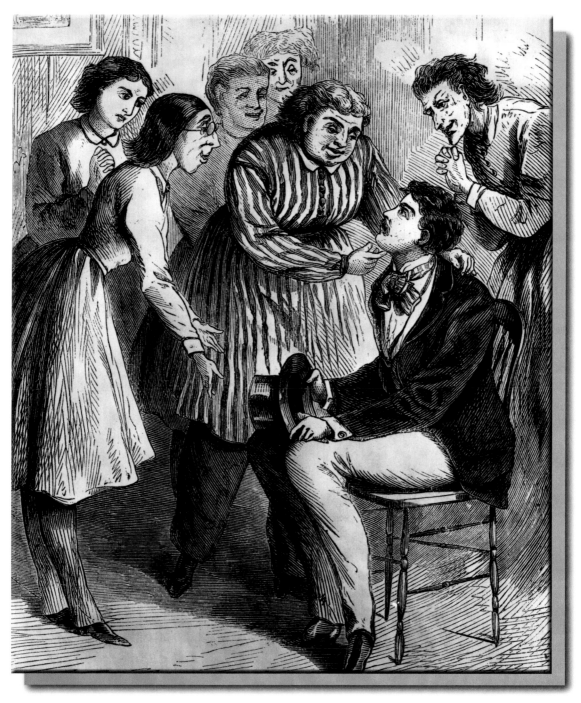

Recruit arriving at the utopian community in Oneida, N.Y. Library of Congress, Washington, D.C.

reminding their materialistic fellow citizens that the American Dream was not yet a reality, pointing to the gulf between the ideal and the actuality.

RELIGIOUS-INSPIRED REFORM

Notwithstanding the wide impact of the American version of secular perfectionism, it was the reform inspired by religious zeal that was most apparent in the antebellum United States. Not that religious enthusiasm was invariably identified with social uplift; many reformers were more concerned with saving souls than with curing social ills. The merchant princes who played active roles in—and donated large sums of money to—the Sunday school unions, home missionary

Brook Farm

Lasting from 1841 to 1847, the Brook Farm Institute of Agriculture and Education was a short-lived utopian experiment in communal living. The 175-acre farm was located in West Roxbury, Mass. (now in Boston). It was organized and virtually directed by George Ripley, a former Unitarian minister, editor of *The Dial* (a critical literary monthly), and a leader in the Transcendental Club, an informal gathering of intellectuals of the Boston area. He was aided by his wife, Sophia Dana Ripley, a woman of wide culture and academic experience.

According to the articles of agreement, Brook Farm was to combine the thinker and the worker, to guarantee the greatest mental freedom, and to prepare a society of liberal, cultivated persons, whose relations with each other would permit a more wholesome and simpler life than could be led amid the pressure of competitive institutions.

The project was financed by the sale of stock, a purchaser of one share automatically becoming a member of the institute, which was governed by a board of directors. The profits, if any, were divided into a number of shares corresponding to the total number of man-days of labour, every member entitled to one share for each day's labour performed. Among the original shareholders were journalist Charles A. Dana and author Nathaniel Hawthorne, who served together as the first directors of agriculture. Ralph Waldo Emerson, Bronson Alcott, Margaret Fuller, Elizabeth Peabody, Theodore Parker, and Orestes A. Brownson were among its interested visitors.

Brook Farm attracted not only intellectuals—though teachers were always in preponderance among the 70 or 80 members—but farmers and craftsmen as well. It paid $1 a day for work (physical or mental) to men and women and provided housing, clothing, and food at approximately actual cost to all members and their dependents. For four years the commune published *The Harbinger*, a weekly magazine devoted to social and political problems, to which James Russell Lowell, John Greenleaf Whittier, and Horace Greeley occasionally contributed.

Brook Farm was noted particularly for the modern educational theory of its excellent school, which sought to establish "perfect freedom of relations between students and teaching body." Discipline at the school was never punitive; rather, it consisted of a gentle attempt to instill in the student a sense of personal responsibility and to communicate a passion for intellectual work.

There were no prescribed study hours, and each student was required to give a few hours a day to manual labour. There was an infant school, a primary school, and a college preparatory course covering six years. Although communal living proved to have disadvantages (Hawthorne found that he was unable to write there and left after six months), for a while it seemed that the ideal of the founders would be realized. Within three years the community—or "Phalanx," as it was called after 1844, when Brook Farm adopted some of the theories of the French Socialist Charles Fourier—had added four houses, workrooms, and dormitories. It then put all available funds into the construction of a large central building to be known as the Phalanstery, which burned to the ground as its completion was being celebrated. Though the colony struggled on for a while, the enterprise gradually failed; the land and buildings were sold in 1849. Ripley worked as the literary critic on Greeley's *New York Tribune* until his death in 1880.

Brook Farm was one of many experiments in communal living that took place in the United States during the first half of the 19th century; it is better known than most and has a secure place in U.S. social history because of the distinguished literary figures and intellectual leaders associated with it. Hawthorne's *Blithedale Romance* (1852) is a fictional treatment of some aspects of the Brook Farm setting.

societies, and Bible and tract societies did so in part out of altruism and in part because the latter organizations stressed spiritual rather than social improvement while teaching the doctrine of the "contented poor." In effect, conservatives who were strongly religious found no difficulty in using religious institutions to fortify their social predilections. Radicals, on the other hand, interpreted Christianity as a call to social action, convinced that true Christian rectitude could be achieved only in struggles that infuriated the smug and the greedy. Ralph Waldo Emerson was an example of the American reformer's insistence on the primacy of the individual. The great goal according to him was the regeneration of the human spirit, rather than a mere improvement in material conditions. Emerson and reformers like him, however, acted on the premise that a foolish consistency was indeed the hobgoblin of little minds, for they saw no contradiction in uniting with like-minded idealists to act out or argue for a new social model. The spirit was to be revived and strengthened through forthright social action undertaken by similarly independent individuals.

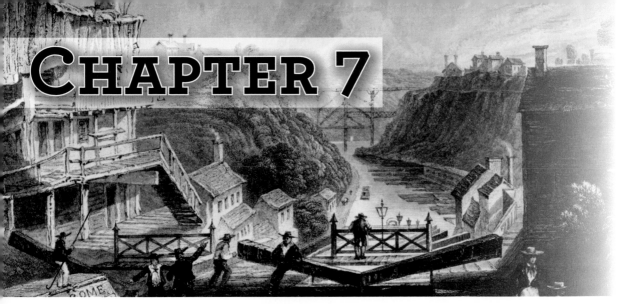

CHAPTER 7

EXPANSIONISM AND POLITICAL CRISIS AT MID-CENTURY

Throughout the 19th century, eastern settlers kept spilling over into the Mississippi Valley and beyond, pushing the frontier farther westward. The Louisiana Purchase territory offered ample room to pioneers and those who came after. American wanderlust, however, was not confined to that area. Throughout the era Americans in varying numbers moved into regions south, west, and north of the Louisiana Territory. Because Mexico and Great Britain held or claimed most of these lands, dispute inevitably broke out between these governments and the United States.

WESTWARD EXPANSION

The growing nationalism of the American people was effectively engaged by the Democratic presidents Jackson and James K. Polk (served 1845–49) and by the expansionist Whig president John Tyler (served 1841–45) to promote their goal of enlarging the "empire for liberty." Each of these presidents performed shrewdly. Jackson waited until his last day in office to establish formal relations with the Republic of Texas, one year after his friend Sam Houston had succeeded in dissolving the ties between Mexico and the newly independent state of Texas. On the Senate's overwhelming repudiation of his proposed treaty of annexation, Tyler resorted to the use of a joint resolution so that each house could vote by a narrow margin for incorporation of Texas into the Union. Polk succeeded in getting the British to negotiate a treaty (1846) whereby the Oregon country south of the 49th parallel would revert to the United States. These were precisely the terms of his earlier proposal, which had been rejected by the British. Ready to resort to almost any means to secure the Mexican territories of New Mexico and upper California, Polk used a border incident as a pretext for commencing a war with Mexico. The Mexican-American War was not widely acclaimed, and many congressmen disliked it, but few dared to oppose the appropriations that financed it.

Although there is no evidence that these actions had anything like a public mandate, clearly they did not evoke widespread opposition. Nonetheless, the expansionists' assertion that Polk's election in 1844 could be construed as a popular clamour for the annexation of Texas was hardly a solid claim; Clay was narrowly defeated and would have won but for the defection from Whig ranks of small numbers of Liberty Party and

John Tyler. Library of Congress, Washington, D.C.

nativist voters. The nationalistic idea, conceived in the 1840s by a Democratic editor, that it was the "manifest destiny" of the United States to expand westward to the Pacific undoubtedly prepared public opinion for the militant policies undertaken by Polk shortly thereafter. It has been said that this notion represented the mood of the American people; it is safer to say it reflected the feelings of many of the people.

The continuation of westward expansion naturally came at the further expense of the American Indians. The sociocultural environment of "young

James K. Polk. Library of Congress, Washington D.C. (neg. no. LC-USZC4-2115)

America" offered fresh rationales for the dispossession of Native Americans; the broadening of federal power provided administrative machinery to carry it out; and the booming economy spurred the demand to bring ever more "virgin land" still in Indian hands into the orbit of "civilization."

After 1815, control of Indian affairs was shifted from the State Department to the War Department (and subsequently to the Department of the Interior, created in 1849). The Indians were no longer treated as peoples of separate nations but were considered wards of the United States, to be relocated at the convenience of the government when necessary. The acquisition of the Louisiana Territory in 1803 and Florida in 1819 removed the last possibilities of outside help for the Indians from France or Spain; moreover, they opened new areas for "resettlement" of unassimilable population elements.

The decimated and dependent Indian peoples of Michigan, Indiana, Illinois, and Wisconsin were, one after another, forced onto reservations within those states in areas that Americans of European descent

Document: John L. O'Sullivan: Our Manifest Destiny (1845)

The phrase "manifest destiny" both defined and encouraged the spirit of expansionism and was used to promote and to justify the spread of democracy across the North American continent. The phrase was probably coined by John O'Sullivan, the editor of the United States Magazine and Democratic Review, *and was first used by him in an editorial in July 1845 calling for the annexation of Texas. Sections of the article appear below. It was used again by O'Sullivan in the Dec. 27, 1845, issue of another paper that he edited, the* New York Morning News, *this time to prove that the United States had "true title" to the Oregon Territory. It was in the context of the Oregon question that the phrase gained wide currency, first in Congress and then in the general press.*

It is time now for opposition to the annexation of Texas to cease, all further agitation of the waters of bitterness and strife, at least in connection with this question, even though it may perhaps be required of us as a necessary condition of the freedom of our institutions, that we must live on forever in a state of unpausing struggle and excitement upon some subject of party division or other. But, in regard to Texas, enough has now been given to party. It is time for the common duty of patriotism to the country to succeed; or if this claim will not be recognized, it is at least time for common sense to acquiesce with decent grace in the inevitable and the irrevocable.

Texas is now ours. Already, before these words are written, her convention has undoubtedly ratified the acceptance, by her congress, of our proffered invitation into the Union; and made the requisite changes in her already republican form of constitution to adapt it to its future federal relations. Her star and her stripe may already be said to have taken their place in the glorious blazon of our common nationality; and the sweep of our eagle's wing already includes within its circuit the wide extent of her fair and fertile land.

She is no longer to us a mere geographical space—a certain combination of coast, plain, mountain, valley, forest, and stream. She is no longer to us a mere country on the map. She comes within the dear and sacred designation of our country; no longer a *pays* [country], she is a part of *la patrie*; and that which is at once a sentiment and a virtue, patriotism, already begins to thrill for her too within the national heart....

did not yet see as valuable. There was almost no resistance, except for the Sauk and Fox uprising led by Black Hawk (the Black Hawk War) in 1832 and put down by local militia whose ranks included a young Abraham Lincoln. It was a slightly different story in the Southeast, where the so-called Five Civilized Tribes (the Chickasaw, Cherokee, Creek, Choctaw, and Seminole peoples) were moving toward assimilation. Many individual members of these groups had become landholders and even slaveowners. The Cherokee, under the guidance of their outstanding statesman Sequoyah, had even developed a written language and were establishing U.S.-style communal institutions on lands in north Georgia ceded to them by treaty. The Treaty of New Echota was violated by squatters on Indian land, but when the Cherokees went to court— not to war—and won their case in the Supreme Court (*Worcester* v. *Georgia*), Pres. Andrew Jackson supported Georgia in contemptuously ignoring the decision. The national government moved on inexorably toward a policy of resettlement

Chief Black Hawk. Library of Congress, Washington, D.C.

in the Indian Territory (later Oklahoma) beyond the Mississippi, and, after the policy's enactment into law in 1830, the Southeast Indian peoples were driven westward along what came to be known as the Trail of Tears. The Seminole, however, resisted and fought the seven-year-long Second Seminole War in the swamps of Florida before the inevitable surrender in 1842.

That a policy of "population transfer" foreshadowing some of the later totalitarian infamies of the 20th century should be so readily embraced in democratic 19th-century America is comprehensible in the light of cultural forces. The revival-inspired missionary movement, while Native American-friendly in theory, assumed that the cultural integrity of Indian land would and should disappear when the Indians were "brought to Christ." A romantic sentimentalization of the "noble red man," evidenced in the literary works of James Fenimore Cooper

Document: Andrew Jackson: On Indian Removal (1830)

In the following message to Congress on Dec. 6, 1830, Pres. Andrew Jackson inaugurated the policy of extinguishing all Indian title to such lands and removing Native Americans to an area beyond the Mississippi River. The president asserted that such a policy would avoid a "collision" between federal authority over Native Americans and state jurisdiction of their lands, and that it would open to "dense and civilized population" areas previously occupied only by "a few savage hunters." The policy was upheld by the Supreme Court in the case of Cherokee Nation v. State of Georgia, *but when Chief Justice John Marshall ruled in* Worcester v. Georgia *that the Indians retained certain rights in their own lands, Jackson is said to have retorted, "John Marshall has made his decision, now let him enforce it."*

It gives me pleasure to announce to Congress that the benevolent policy of the government, steadily pursued for nearly thirty years, in relation to the removal of the Indians beyond the white settlements is approaching to a happy consummation. Two important tribes have accepted the provision made for their removal at the last session of Congress, and it is believed that their example will induce the remaining tribes also to seek the same obvious advantages.

The consequences of a speedy removal will be important to the United States, to individual states, and to the Indians themselves. The pecuniary advantages which it promises to the government are the least of its recommendations. It puts an end to all possible danger of collision between the authorities of the general and state governments on account of the Indians. It will place a dense and civilized population in large tracts of country now occupied by a few savage hunters. By opening the whole territory between Tennessee on the north and Louisiana on the south to the settlement of the whites it will incalculably strengthen the southwestern frontier and render the adjacent states strong enough to repel future invasions without remote aid. It will relieve the whole state of Mississippi and the western part of Alabama of Indian occupancy, and enable those states to advance rapidly in population, wealth, and power....

and Henry Wadsworth Longfellow, called attention to positive aspects of Indian life but saw Native Americans as essentially a vanishing breed. Far more common in American thought was the concept of the "treacherous redskin," which lifted Jackson and William Henry Harrison to the presidency in 1828 and 1840, respectively, partly on the strength of their military victories over Indians. Popular celebration of allegedly Anglo-Saxon characteristics of energy and independence helped to brand other "races"—Indians as well as Africans, Asians, and Hispanics—as inferiors who would have to yield to progress. In all, the historical moment was unkind to the Indians, as some of the values that in fact did sustain the growth and prosperity of the United States were the same ones that worked against any live-and-let-live arrangement between the original Americans and the newcomers.

ATTITUDES TOWARD EXPANSIONISM

Public attitudes toward expansion into Mexican territories were very much affected by the issue of slavery. Those opposed to the spread of slavery or simply not in favour of the institution joined abolitionists in discerning a proslavery policy in the Mexican-American War. The great political issue of the postwar years concerned slavery in the territories. Calhoun and spokesmen for the slave-owning South argued that slavery could not be constitutionally prohibited in the Mexican cession.

Document: Territorial Expansion and the Extension of Slavery (1847)

In August 1846 Pennsylvania congressman David Wilmot moved that a proviso barring slavery from the territories acquired as a result of the Mexican War be attached to an appropriations bill being discussed in the House of Representatives. Although never passed, the Wilmot Proviso was reintroduced on several occasions and ignited a political war that helped bring about the deterioration of both major parties. Northern Whigs and radical Democrats united to support the Proviso, while Conservative Democrats and Southern Whigs denounced it. Sen. John C. Calhoun denied the right of Congress to exclude slavery from the territories, and in the editorial that follows, his arguments were endorsed. The editorial also endorsed the vigorously expansionist "all Mexico movement."

The war, which the insane folly of the Spaniards has forced upon us after fifty years of threatening and surrendering of territory reluctantly as we have pressed upon their front, has the disadvantage of acquiring territory too fast, "before our population is sufficiently advanced to gain it from them piece by piece." That was a wise policy ascribed in the early stages of the war to Almonte and his party, who, learning more from the experience of the past than our own politicians have done, saw in the last fifty years of peace the steady and resistless approach of the

American people. They saw territory after territory, no matter by whom owned or by what people inhabited, swallowed up in the great Union, the march of which was not perceptibly stayed, even when Louisiana and its French citizens became an American republic. They saw Texas suddenly grow into a state through Anglo-Saxon energy, and as promptly fall into the line of the Union, while its pioneers were already taking root in California and New Mexico....

"Free Soilers" supported the Wilmot Proviso idea—that slavery should not be permitted in the new territory. Others supported the proposal that popular sovereignty (called "squatter sovereignty" by its detractors) should prevail—that is, that settlers in the territories should decide the issue. Still others called for the extension westward of the 36°30′ line of demarcation for slavery that had resolved the Missouri controversy in 1820. Now, 30 years later, Clay again pressed a compromise on the country, supported dramatically by the aging Daniel Webster and by moderates in and out of the Congress. As the events in the California gold fields showed (beginning in 1849), many people had things other than political principles on their minds. The Compromise of 1850, as the separate resolutions resolving the controversy came to be known, infuriated those of high principle on both sides of the issue—Southerners resented that the compromise admitted California as a free state, abolished the slave trade in the District of Columbia, and gave territories the theoretical right to deny existence to their "peculiar institution," while antislavery men deplored the same theoretical right of territories to permit the institution and abhorred the new, more-stringent federal fugitive-slave law. That Southern political leaders ceased talking secession shortly after the enactment of the compromise indicates who truly won the political skirmish. The people probably approved the settlement—but as subsequent events were to show, the issues had not been met but had been only deferred.

CONCLUSION

By canal, by steamboat, by train, and by fiat, the United States of America spread out farther across the continent in the first half of the 19th century. At the same time, the dawn of industrialism brought the factory system to cities that grew exponentially, becoming home to burgeoning numbers of labourers and immigrants who were often one and the same. Markets expanded, and the economy became more integrated. Southern plantations grew cotton that New England textile mills finished, and the West manufactured promise. Inventors and entrepreneurs flourished. Fortunes were made.

In the age of Andrew Jackson, the country had definitely become more Democratic—that party having vanquished its Federalist rivals—but it also seemed to be becoming more *democratic*, as the vote was extended to an increasing number of Americans, including a growing number of those who did not own property. By and large, however, the so-called Era of the Common Man was not nearly as good as advertised for common Americans, though those at the top of the socioeconomic pyramid thrived. Yet this was also an era in which a spate of reform movements sought real political and economic democracy for women, for working people, and for the enslaved.

It was truly an Era of Mixed Feelings. Certainly, neither Mexico nor Native Americans saw it as the manifest destiny of the United States to expand to the Pacific. Most of those in the South were determined that new territories and states be open to slavery; most of those in the North were equally determined that they not be. The gap between regions and between rich and poor was widening. Accommodation may have been found in the Missouri Compromise of 1820 and the Compromise of 1850, but as the country moved into the second half of the century, talk became cheaper and the price of compromise too high.

Appendix: Primary Source Documents

JAMES MONROE: THE MONROE DOCTRINE (1823)

A Compilation of the Messages and Papers of the Presidents 1789-1897, James D. Richardson, ed., Washington, 1896–99, Vol. II, pp. 207–220.

A precise knowledge of our relations with foreign powers as respects our negotiations and transactions with each is thought to be particularly necessary. ...

At the proposal of the Russian Imperial government, made through the minister of the emperor residing here, full power and instructions have been transmitted to the minister of the United States at St. Petersburg to arrange by amicable negotiation the respective rights and interests of the two nations on the northwest coast of this continent. A similar proposal had been made by His Imperial Majesty to the government of Great Britain, which has likewise been acceded to. The government of the United States has been desirous, by this friendly proceeding, of manifesting the great value which they have invariably attached to the friendship of the emperor and their solicitude to cultivate the best understanding with his government.

In the discussions to which this interest has given rise and in the arrangements by which they may terminate the occasion has been judged proper for asserting, as a principle in which the rights and interests of the United States are involved, that the American continents, by the free and independent condition which they have assumed and maintain, are henceforth not to be considered as subjects for future colonization by any European powers. ...

It was stated at the commencement of the last session that great effort was then making in Spain and Portugal to improve the condition of the people of those countries and that it appeared to be conducted with extraordinary moderation. It need scarcely be remarked that the result has been so far very different from what was then anticipated. Of events in that quarter of the globe with which we have so much intercourse and from which we derive our origin, we have always been anxious and interested spectators. The citizens of the United States cherish sentiments the most friendly in favor of the liberty and happiness of their fellowmen on that side of the Atlantic. In the wars of the European powers in matters relating to themselves we have never taken any part, nor does it comport with our policy so to do. It is only when our rights are invaded or seriously menaced that we resent injuries or make preparation for our defense.

With the movements in this hemisphere we are of necessity more immediately connected, and by causes which must be obvious to all enlightened and impartial observers. The political system of the allied powers is essentially different in this respect from that of America. This difference proceeds from that which exists in their respective governments; and to the defense of our own, which has been achieved by the loss of so much blood and treasure, and matured by the wisdom of their most enlightened citizens, and under which we have enjoyed unexampled felicity, this whole nation is devoted. We owe it, therefore, to candor and to the amicable relations existing between the United States and those powers to declare that we should consider any attempt on their part to extend their system to any portion of this hemisphere as dangerous to our peace and safety.

With the existing colonies or dependencies of any European power we have not interfered and shall not interfere. But with the governments who have declared their independence and maintained it, and whose independence we have, on great consideration and on just principles, acknowledged, we could not view any interposition for the purpose of oppressing them, or controlling in any other manner their destiny, by any European power in any other light than as the manifestation of an unfriendly disposition toward the United States. In the war between those new governments and Spain we declared our neutrality at the time of their recognition, and to this we have adhered, and shall continue to adhere, provided no change shall occur which, in the judgment of the competent authorities of this government, shall make a corresponding change on the part of the United States indispensable to their security.

The late events in Spain and Portugal show that Europe is still unsettled. Of this important fact no stronger proof can be adduced than that the allied powers should have thought it proper, on any principle satisfactory to themselves, to have interposed by force in the internal concerns of Spain. To what extent such interposition may be carried, on the same principle, is a question in which all independent powers whose governments differ from theirs are interested, even those most remote, and surely none more so than the United States.

Our policy in regard to Europe, which was adopted at an early stage of the wars which have so long agitated that quarter of the globe, nevertheless remains the same, which is not to interfere in the internal concerns of any of its powers; to consider the government de facto as the legitimate government for us; to cultivate friendly relations with it, and to preserve those relations by a frank, firm, and manly policy, meeting in all instances the just claims of every power, submitting to injuries from none. But in regard to those continents, circumstances are eminently and conspicuously different. It is impossible that the allied powers should extend their political system to any portion of either continent without endangering our peace and happiness; nor can anyone believe that our southern brethren, if left to themselves, would adopt it of their own accord.

It is equally impossible, therefore, that we should behold such interposition in any form with indifference. If we look to the comparative strength and resources of Spain and those new governments, and their distance from each other, it must be obvious that she can never subdue them. It is still the true policy of the United States to leave the parties to themselves, in the hope that other powers will pursue the same course.

JOHN MARSHALL: *DARTMOUTH COLLEGE V. WOODWARD* (1819)

Reports of Cases Argued and Adjudged in the Supreme Court of the United States, Henry Wheaton, ed., New York, 1819, Vol. 4, p. 624ff.

It can require no argument to prove that the circumstances of this case constitute a contract. An application is made to the Crown for a charter to incorporate a religious and literary institution. In the application it is stated that large contributions have been made for the object, which will be conferred on the corporation as soon as it shall be created. The charter is granted, and on its faith the property is conveyed. Surely in this transaction every ingredient of a complete and legitimate contract is to be found.

The points for consideration are:

- Is this contract protected by the Constitution of the United States?
- Is it impaired by the acts under which the defendant holds?

On the first point, it has been argued that the word "contract," in its broadest sense, would comprehend the political relations between the government and its citizens, would extend to offices held within a state for state purposes and to many of those laws concerning civil institutions, which must change with circumstances and be modified by ordinary legislation; which deeply concern the public, and which, to preserve good government, the public judgment must control — that even marriage is a contract, and its obligations are affected by the laws respecting divorces; that the clause in the Constitution, if construed in its greatest latitude, would prohibit these laws.

Taken in its broad, unlimited sense, the clause would be an unprofitable and vexatious interference with the internal concerns of a state, would unnecessarily and unwisely embarrass its legislation, and render immutable those civil institutions which are established for purposes of internal government, and which, to subserve those purposes, ought to vary with varying circumstances. That as the framers of the Constitution could never have intended to insert in that instrument a provision so unnecessary, so mischievous, and so repugnant to its general spirit, the term "contract" must be understood in a more limited sense. That it must be understood as intended to guard against a power of at least doubtful utility, the abuse of which had been extensively felt; and to restrain the legislature in future from violating the right to property. That anterior to the formation of the Constitution, a course of legislation had prevailed in many, if not in all, of the states which weakened the confidence of man in man and embarrassed all transactions between individuals by dispensing with a faithful performance of engagements.

To correct this mischief, by restraining the power which produced it, the state legislatures were forbidden "to pass any law impairing the obligation of contracts," that is, of contracts respecting property, under which some individual could claim a right to something beneficial to himself; and that since the clause in the Constitution must in construction receive some limitation, it may be confined, and ought to be confined, to cases of this description; to cases within the mischief it was intended to remedy....

The provision of the Constitution never has been understood to embrace other contracts than those which respect property, or some object of value, and confer rights which may be asserted in a court of justice. It never has been understood to restrict the general right of the legislature to legislate on the subject of divorces. Those acts enable some tribunal not to impair a marriage contract but to liberate one of the parties because it has been broken by the other. When any state legislature shall pass an act annulling all marriage contracts, or allowing either party to annul it without the consent of the other, it will be time enough to inquire whether such an act be constitutional.

The parties in this case differ less on general principles, less on the true construction of the Constitution in the abstract than on the application of those principles to this case and on the true construction of the charter of 1769. This is the point on which the cause essentially depends. If the act of incorporation be a grant of political power, if it create a civil institution to be employed in the administration of the government, or if the funds of the college be public property, or if the state of New Hampshire, as a government, be alone interested in its transactions, the subject is one in which the legislature of the state may act according to its own judgment, unrestrained by any limitation of its power imposed by the Constitution of the United States.

But if this be a private, eleemosynary institution, endowed with a capacity to take property for objects unconnected with government, whose funds are bestowed by individuals on the faith of the charter; if the donors have stipulated for the future disposition and management of those funds in the manner prescribed by themselves, there may be more difficulty in the case, although neither the persons who have made these stipulations nor those for whose benefit they were made should be parties to the cause. Those who are no longer interested in the property may yet retain such an interest in the preservation of their own arrangements as to have a right to insist that those arrangements shall be held sacred. Or, if they have themselves disappeared, it becomes a subject of serious and anxious inquiry whether those whom they have legally empowered to represent them forever may not assert all the rights which they possessed, while in being; whether, if they be without personal representatives who may feel injured by a violation of the compact, the trustees be not so completely their representatives, in the eye of the law, as to stand in their place, not only as respects the government of the college but also as respects the maintenance of the college charter....

A corporation is an artificial being, invisible, intangible, and existing only in contemplation of law. Being the mere creature of law, it possesses only those properties which the charter of its creation confers upon it, either expressly or as incidental to its very existence. These are such as are supposed best calculated to effect the object for which it was created. Among the most important are immortality, and, if the expression may be allowed, individuality; properties by which a perpetual succession of many persons are considered as the same, and may act as a single individual. They enable a corporation to manage its own affairs and to hold property without the perplexing intricacies, the hazardous and endless necessity of perpetual conveyances for the purpose of transmitting it from hand to hand. It is chiefly for the purpose of clothing bodies of men, in succession, with these qualities and capacities that corporations were invented and are in use.

By these means, a perpetual succession of individuals are capable of acting for the promotion of the particular object,

like one immortal being. But this being does not share in the civil government of the country, unless that be the purpose for which it was created. Its immortality no more confers on it political power, or a political character, than immortality would confer such power or character on a natural person. It is no more a state instrument than a natural person exercising the same powers would be.

If, then, a natural person, employed by individuals in the education of youth, or for the government of a seminary in which youth is educated, would not become a public officer, or be considered as a member of the civil government, how is it that this artificial being, created by law for the purpose of being employed by the same individuals for the same purposes, should become a part of the civil government of the country? Is it because its existence, its capacities, its powers are given by law? Because the government has given it the power to take and to hold property in a particular form, and for particular purposes, has the government a consequent right substantially to change that form or to vary the purposes to which the property is to be applied? This principle has never been asserted or recognized and is supported by no authority. Can it derive aid from reason?...

From the fact, then, that a charter of incorporation has been granted, nothing can be inferred which changes the character of the institution or transfers to the government any new power over it. The character of civil institutions does not grow out of their incorporation but out of the manner in which they are formed and the objects for which they are created. The right to change them is not founded on their being incorporated but on their being the instruments of government, created for its purposes. The same institutions, created for the same objects though not incorporated, would be public institutions and, of course, be controllable by the legislature. The incorporating act neither gives nor prevents this control. Neither, in reason, can the incorporating act change the character of a private, eleemosynary institution....

From this review of the charter, it appears that Dartmouth College is an eleemosynary institution, incorporated for the purpose of perpetuating the application of the bounty of the donors to the specified objects of that bounty; that its trustees or governors were originally named by the founder and invested with the power of perpetuating themselves; that they are not public officers, nor is it a civil institution, participating in the administration of government, but a charity school, or a seminary of education, incorporated for the preservation of its property, and the perpetual application of that property to the objects of its creation.

Yet a question remains to be considered, of more real difficulty, on which more doubt has been entertained than on all that have been discussed. The founders of the college, at least those whose contributions were in money, have parted with the property bestowed upon it, and their representatives have no interest in that property. The donors of land are equally without interest so long as the corporation shall exist. Could they be found, they are unaffected by any alteration in its constitution, and probably regardless of its form, or even of its existence. The students are fluctuating, and no individual among our youth has a vested interest in the institution, which can be asserted in a court of justice. Neither the founders of the college nor the youth for whose benefit it was founded, complain of the alteration made in its charter or think themselves injured by it. The trustees alone complain, and the trustees have no beneficial interest to be protected. Can this be such a contract, as the constitution intended to withdraw from the power of state legislation? Contracts, the parties to which have a vested beneficial interest, and those only, it has been said, are the objects about which the Constitution is solicitous, and to which its protection is extended....

According to the theory of the British constitution, their Parliament is omnipotent. To annul corporate rights might give a shock to public opinion, which that government has chosen to avoid; but its power is not questioned. Had Parliament, immediately after the emanation of this charter, and the execution of those conveyances which followed it, annulled the instrument, so that the living donors would have witnessed the disappointment of their hopes, the perfidy of the transaction would have been universally acknowledged. Yet then, as now, the donors would have had no interest in the property; then, as now, those who might be students would have had no rights to be violated; then, as now, it might be said that the trustees, in whom the rights of all were combined, possessed no private, individual, beneficial interest in the property confided to their protection. Yet the contract would at that time have been deemed sacred by all. What has since occurred to strip it of its inviolability? Circumstances have not changed it. In reason, in justice, and in law, it is now what it was in 1769.

This is plainly a contract to which the donors, the trustees, and the Crown (to whose rights and obligations New Hampshire succeeds) were the original parties. It is a contract made on a valuable consideration. It is a contract for the security and disposition of property. It is a contract on the faith of which real and personal estate has been conveyed to the corporation. It is then a contract within the letter of the Constitution, and within its spirit also, unless the fact that the property is invested by the donors in trustees for the promotion of religion and education, for the benefit of persons who are perpetually changing, though the objects remain the same, shall create a particular exception, taking this case out of the prohibition contained in the Constitution.

It is more than possible that the preservation of rights of this description was not particularly in the view of the framers of the Constitution when the clause under consideration was introduced into that instrument. It is probable that interferences of more frequent recurrence, to which the temptation was stronger and of which the mischief was more extensive, constituted the great motive for imposing this restriction on the state legislatures. But although a particular and a rare case may not, in itself, be of sufficient magnitude to induce a rule, yet it must be governed by the rule, when established, unless some plain and strong reason for excluding it can be given.

It is not enough to say that this particular case was not in the mind of the Convention when the article was framed, nor of the American people when it was adopted. It is necessary to go further and to say that, had this particular case been suggested, the language would have been so varied as to exclude it, or it would have been made a special exception. The case, being within the words of the rule, must be within its operation likewise, unless there be something in the literal construction so obviously absurd, or mischievous, or repugnant to the general spirit of the instrument as to justify those who expound the Constitution in making it an exception.

On what safe and intelligible ground can this exception stand? There is no expression in the Constitution, no sentiment delivered by its contemporaneous expounders which would justify us in making it. In the absence of all authority of this kind, is there, in the nature and reason of the case itself, that which would sustain a construction of the Constitution not warranted by its words? Are contracts of this description of a character to excite so little interest that we must exclude them from the provisions of the Constitution as being unworthy of the attention of those who framed the instrument? Or does public policy so imperiously demand their remaining exposed to legislative alteration as to compel us, or rather permit us, to say that these words, which were introduced to give stability to contracts, and which in their plain import comprehend this contract, must yet be so construed as to exclude it?

Almost all eleemosynary corporations, those which are created for the promotion of religion, of charity, or of education, are of the same character. The law of this case is the law of all. In every literary or charitable institution, unless the objects of the bounty be themselves incorporated, the whole legal interest is in trustees and can be asserted only by them. The donors, or claimants of the bounty, if they can appear in court at all, can appear only to complain of the trustees. In all other situations, they are identified with, and personated by, the trustees; and their rights are to be defended and maintained by them. Religion, charity, and education are, in the law of England, legatees or donees, capable of receiving bequests or donations in this form. They appear in court and claim or defend by the corporation. ...

The opinion of the Court, after mature deliberation, is that this is a contract, the obligation of which cannot be impaired without violating the Constitution of the United States. This opinion appears to us to be equally supported by reason and by the former decisions of this Court.

We next proceed to the inquiry whether its obligation has been impaired by those acts of the legislature of New Hampshire to which the special verdict refers....

By the Revolution, the duties as well as the powers of government devolved on the people of New Hampshire. It is admitted that among the latter was comprehended the transcendent power of Parliament, as well as that of the Executive Department. It is too clear to require the support of argument that all contracts and rights respecting property remained unchanged by the Revolution.

The obligations, then, which were created by the charter to Dartmouth College were the same in the new that they had been in the old government. The power of the government was also the same. A repeal of this charter at any time prior to the adoption of the present Constitution of the United States would have been an extraordinary and unprecedented act of power, but one which could have been contested only by the restrictions upon the legislature to be found in the constitution of the state. But the Constitution of the United States has imposed this additional limitation, that the legislature of a state shall pass no act "impairing the obligation of contracts."

It has been already stated that the act "to amend the charter, and enlarge and improve the corporation of Dartmouth College" increases the number of trustees to twenty-one, gives the appointment of the additional members to the executive of the state, and creates a board of overseers to consist of twenty-five persons, of whom twenty-one are also appointed by the executive of New Hampshire, who have power to inspect and control the most important acts of the trustees.

On the effect of this law, two opinions cannot be entertained. Between acting directly and acting through the agency of trustees and overseers, no essential difference is perceived. The whole power of governing the college is transferred from trustees, appointed according to the will of the founder, expressed in the charter, to the executive of New Hampshire. The management and application of the funds of this eleemosynary institution, which are placed by the donors in the hands of trustees named in the charter and empowered to perpetuate themselves, are placed by this act under the control of the government of the state. The will of the state is substituted for the will of the donors in every essential operation of the college.

This is not an immaterial change. The founders of the college contracted, not merely for the perpetual application of the funds which they gave to the objects for which those funds were given; they contracted, also, to secure that application by the constitution of the corporation. They contracted for a system, which should, as far as human foresight can provide, retain forever the government of the literary institution they had formed in the hands of persons approved by themselves.

This system is totally changed. The charter of 1769 exists no longer. It is

reorganized; and reorganized in such a manner as to convert a literary institution, molded according to the will of its founders and placed under the control of private literary men, into a machine entirely subservient to the will of government. This may be for the advantage of this college in particular, and may be for the advantage of literature in general, but it is not according to the will of the donors, and is subversive of that contract, on the faith of which their property was given.

In the view which has been taken of this interesting case, the Court has confined itself to the rights possessed by the trustees, as the assignees and representatives of the donors and founders, for the benefit of religion and literature. Yet it is not clear that the trustees ought to be considered as destitute of such beneficial interest in themselves as the law may respect. In addition to their being the legal owners of the property, and to their having a freehold right in the powers confided to them, the charter itself countenances the idea that trustees may also be tutors with salaries. The first president was one of the original trustees; and the charter provides that in case of vacancy in that office "the senior professor or tutor, *being one of the trustees,* shall exercise the office of president until the trustees shall make choice of, and appoint a president."

According to the tenor of the charter, then, the trustees might, without impropriety, appoint a president and other professors from their own body. This is a power not entirely unconnected with an interest. Even if the proposition of the counsel for the defendant were sustained; if it were admitted that those contracts only are protected by the Constitution, a beneficial interest in which is vested in the party, who appears in court to assert that interest; yet it is by no means clear that the trustees of Dartmouth College have no beneficial interest in themselves. But the Court has deemed it unnecessary to investigate this particular point....

It results from this opinion that the acts of the legislature of New Hampshire, which are stated in the special verdict found in this cause, are repugnant to the Constitution of the United States; and that the judgment on this special verdict ought to have been for the plaintiffs. The judgment of the state court must therefore be reversed.

JOHN QUINCY ADAMS: SLAVERY AND THE CONSTITUTION (1820)

Memoirs of John Quincy Adams, Comprising Portions of His Diary from 1795 to 1848, Charles Francis Adams, ed., Vol. V, Philadelphia, 1875, pp. 4–12.

When I came this day to my office, I found there a note requesting me to call at one o'clock at the President's house. It was then one, and I immediately went over. He expected that the two bills—for the admission of Maine, and to enable Missouri to make a constitution—would have been brought to him for his signature, and he had summoned all the members of the administration to ask their opinions, in

writing, to be deposited in the Department of State, upon two questions: (1) whether Congress had a constitutional right to prohibit slavery in a territory; and (2) whether the 8th Section of the Missouri bill (which interdicts slavery *forever* in the territory north of thirty-six and a half latitude) was applicable only to the territorial state, or could extend to it after it should become a state....

After this meeting, I walked home with Calhoun, who said that ... in the Southern country ... domestic labor was confined to the blacks; and such was the prejudice that if he, who was the most popular man in his district, were to keep a white servant in his house, his character and reputation would be irretrievably ruined.

I said that this confounding of the ideas of servitude and labor was one of the bad effects of slavery; but he thought it attended with many excellent consequences. It did not apply to all kinds of labor—not, for example, to farming. He himself had often held the plough; so had his father. Manufacturing and mechanical labor was not degrading. It was only manual labor—the proper work of slaves. No white person could descend to that. And it was the best guarantee to equality among the whites. It produced an unvarying level among them. It not only did not excite but did not even admit of inequalities, by which one white man could domineer over another.

I told Calhoun I could not see things in the same light. It is, in truth, all perverted sentiment—mistaking labor for slavery, and dominion for freedom. The discussion of this Missouri question has betrayed the secret of their souls. In the abstract they admit that slavery is an evil, they disclaim all participation in the introduction of it, and cast it all upon the shoulders of our old Grandam Britain. But when probed to the quick upon it, they show at the bottom of their souls pride and vainglory in their condition of masterdom. They fancy themselves more generous and noblehearted than the plain freemen who labor for subsistence. They look down upon the simplicity of a Yankee's manners, because he has no habits of overbearing like theirs and cannot treat Negroes like dogs.

It is among the evils of slavery that it taints the very sources of moral principle. It establishes false estimates of virtue and vice; for what can be more false and heartless than this doctrine which makes the first and holiest rights of humanity to depend upon the color of the skin? It perverts human reason, and reduces man endowed with logical powers to maintain that slavery is sanctioned by the Christian religion, that slaves are happy and contented in their condition, that between master and slave there are ties of mutual attachment and affection, that the virtues of the master are refined and exalted by the degradation of the slave; while at the same time they vent execrations upon the slave trade, curse Britain for having given them slaves, burn at the stake Negroes convicted of crimes for the terror of the example, and writhe in agonies of fear at the very mention of human rights as applicable to men of color. The

impression produced upon my mind by the progress of this discussion is that the bargain between freedom and slavery contained in the Constitution of the United States is morally and politically vicious, inconsistent with the principles upon which alone our Revolution can be justified; cruel and oppressive, by riveting the chains of slavery, by pledging the faith of freedom to maintain and perpetuate the tyranny of the master; and grossly unequal and impolitic, by admitting that slaves are at once enemies to be kept in subjection, property to be secured or restored to their owners, and persons not to be represented themselves, but for whom their masters are privileged with nearly a double share of representation. The consequence has been that this slave representation has governed the Union.

Benjamin portioned above his brethren has ravined as a wolf. In the morning he has devoured the prey, and at night he has divided the spoil. It would be no difficult matter to prove, by reviewing the history of the Union under this Constitution, that almost everything which has contributed to the honor and welfare of the nation has been accomplished in spite of them or forced upon them, and that everything unpropitious and dishonorable, including the blunders and follies of their adversaries, may be traced to them.

I have favored this Missouri Compromise, believing it to be all that could be effected under the present Constitution, and from extreme unwillingness to put the Union at hazard. But perhaps it would have been a wiser as well as a bolder course to have persisted in the restriction upon Missouri, till it should have terminated in a convention of the states to revise and amend the Constitution. This would have produced a new Union of thirteen or fourteen States, unpolluted with slavery, with a great and glorious object to effect; namely, that of rallying to their standard the other states by the universal emancipation of their slaves. If the Union must be dissolved, slavery is precisely the question upon which it ought to break. For the present, however, this contest is laid asleep.

HENRY CLAY: THE PROTECTIVE TARIFF (1824)

The Works of Henry Clay Comprising His Life, Correspondence and Speeches, Calvin Colton, ed., New York, 1904, Vol. VI, pp. 254–294.

The policy of all Europe is adverse to the reception of our agricultural produce so far as it comes into collision with its own; and, under that limitation, we are absolutely forbid to enter their ports, except under circumstances which deprive them of all value as a steady market. The policy of all Europe rejects those great staples of our country which consist of objects of human subsistence. The policy of all Europe refuses to receive from us anything but those raw materials of smaller value, essential to their manufactures, to which they can give a higher value, with the exception of tobacco and rice, which they cannot produce. Even Great Britain, to which we are its best customer, and from which we receive nearly one half in value of our whole imports, will not take from us articles of subsistence produced in our country cheaper than can be produced in Great Britain....

Is this foreign market, so incompetent at present, and which, limited as its demands are, operates so unequally upon the productive labor of our country, likely to improve in future? If I am correct in the views which I have presented to the committee, it must become worse and worse. What can improve it? Europe will not abandon her own agriculture to foster ours. We may even anticipate that she will more and more enter into competition with us in the supply of the West India market....

Our agriculture is our greatest interest. It ought ever to be predominant. All others should bend to it. And, in considering what is for its advantage, we should contemplate it in all its varieties, of planting, farming, and grazing. Can we do nothing to invigorate it; nothing to correct the errors of the past, and to brighten the still more unpromising prospects which lie before us? We have seen, I think, the causes of the distresses of the country. We have seen that an exclusive dependence upon the foreign market must lead to still severer distress, to impoverishment, to ruin.

We must, then, change somewhat our course. We must give a new direction to some portion of our industry. We must speedily adopt a genuine American policy. Still cherishing the foreign market, let us create also a home market to give further scope to the consumption of the produce of American industry. Let us counteract the policy of foreigners and withdraw the support which we now give to their industry and stimulate that of our own country....

By creating a new and extensive business, then, we would not only give employment to those who want it, and augment the sum of national wealth by all that this new business would create, but we should meliorate the condition of those who are now engaged in existing employments. In Europe, particularly Great Britain, their large standing armies, large navies, large even on their peace arrangement, their established church afford to their population employments which, in that respect, the happier Constitution of our government does not tolerate but in a very limited degree. The peace establishments of our Army and our Navy are extremely small, and I hope ever will be. We have no established church, and I trust never shall have. In proportion as the enterprise of our citizens in public employments is circumscribed should we excite and invigorate it in private pursuits.

The creation of a home market is not only necessary to procure for our agriculture a just reward for its labors but it is indispensable to obtain a supply for our necessary wants. If we cannot sell, we cannot buy. That portion of our population (and we have seen that it is not less than four-fifths), which makes comparatively nothing that foreigners will buy, has nothing to make purchases with from foreigners. It is in vain that we are told of the amount of our exports supplied by the planting interest. They may enable the planting interest to supply all its wants; but they bring no ability to the interests not planting; unless, which cannot be pretended, the planting interest was an adequate vent for the surplus produce of the labor of all other interests.

It is in vain to tantalize us with the greater cheapness of foreign fabrics. There must be an ability to purchase, if an article be obtained, whatever may be the price, high or low, at which it is sold. And a cheap article is as much beyond the grasp of him who has no means to buy as a high one. Even if it were true that the American manufacturer would supply consumption at dearer rates, it is better to have his fabrics than the unattainable foreign fabrics; because it is better to be ill supplied than not supplied at all. A coarse coat which will communicate warmth and cover nakedness is better than no coat.

The superiority of the home market results, first, from its steadiness and comparative certainty at all times; second, from the creation of reciprocal interest; third, from its greater security; and, last, from an ultimate and not distant augmentation of consumption (and consequently of comfort) from increased quantity and reduced prices. But this home market, highly desirable as it is, can only be created and cherished by the *protection* of our own legislation against the inevitable prostration of our industry, which must ensue from the action of *foreign policy and legislation*.... The measure of the wealth of a nation is indicated by the measure of its protection of its industry; and ... the measure of the poverty of a nation is marked by that of the degree in which it neglects and abandons the care of its own industry, leaving it exposed to the action of foreign powers....

Having called the attention of the committee to the present adverse state of our country, and endeavored to point out the causes which have led to it; having shown that similar causes, wherever they exist in other countries, lead to the same adversity in their condition; and having shown that, wherever we find opposite causes prevailing, a high and animating state of national prosperity exists, the committee will agree with me in thinking that it is the solemn duty of government to apply a remedy to the evils which afflict our country, if it can apply one. Is there no remedy within the reach of the government? Are we doomed to behold our industry languish and decay yet more and more?

But there is a remedy, and that remedy consists in modifying our foreign policy, and in adopting a genuine *American system*. We must naturalize the arts in our country; and we must naturalize them by the only means which the wisdom of nations has yet discovered to be effectual — by adequate protection against the otherwise overwhelming influence of foreigners. This is only to be accomplished by the establishment of a tariff, to the consideration of which I am now brought.

And what is this tariff? It seems to have been regarded as a sort of monster, huge and deformed — a wild beast, endowed with tremendous powers of destruction, about to be let loose among our people, if not to devour them, at least to consume their substance. But let us calm our passions and deliberately survey this alarming, this terrific being. The sole object of the tariff is to tax the produce of foreign industry with the view of promoting American industry. The tax is exclusively leveled at foreign industry. That is the avowed and the direct purpose of the tariff. If it subjects any part of American industry to burdens, that is an effect not intended, but is altogether incidental and perfectly voluntary.

It has been treated as an imposition of burdens upon one part of the community, by design, for the benefit of another; as if, in fact, money were taken from the pockets of one portion of the people and put into the pockets of another. But is that a fair representation of it? No man pays the duty assessed on the foreign article by compulsion, but voluntarily; and this voluntary duty, if paid, goes into the common exchequer for the common benefit of all....

But it is said by the honorable gentleman from Virginia that the South, owing to the character of a certain portion of its population, cannot engage in the business of manufacturing.... What is to be done in this conflict? The gentleman would have us abstain from adopting a policy called for by the interest of the greater and freer part of our population.

But is that reasonable? Can it be expected that the interests of the greater part should be made to bend to the condition of the servile part of our population? That, in effect, would be to make us the slaves of slaves....

The existing state of things, indeed, presents a sort of tacit compact between the cotton grower and the British manufacturer, the stipulations of which are, on the part of the cotton grower, that the whole of the United States, the other portions as well as the cotton growing, shall remain open and unrestricted in the consumption of British manufactures; and, on the part of the British manufacturer, that in consideration thereof, he will continue to purchase the cotton of the South. Thus, then, we perceive that the proposed measure instead of sacrificing the South to the other parts of the Union seeks only to preserve them from being absolutely sacrificed under the operation of the tacit compact which I have described.

Supposing the South to be actually incompetent, or disinclined, to embark at all in the business of manufacturing, is not its interest, nevertheless, likely to be promoted by creating a new and an American source of supply for its consumption? Now, foreign powers, and Great Britain principally, have the monopoly of the supply of Southern consumption. If this bill should pass, an American competitor, in the supply of the South, would be raised up, and ultimately, I cannot doubt, that it will be supplied more cheaply and better....

The second objection to the proposed bill is that it will diminish the amount of our exports. It can have no effect upon our exports, except those which are sent to Europe. Except tobacco and rice, we send there nothing but the raw materials. The argument is that Europe will not buy of us if we do not buy of her. The first objection to it is that it calls upon us to look to the question, and to take care of European ability in legislating for American interests. Now, if in legislating for their interests they would consider and provide for our ability, the principle of reciprocity would enjoin us so to regulate our intercourse with them as to leave their ability unimpaired. But I have shown that, in the adoption of their own policy, their inquiry is strictly limited to a consideration of their peculiar interests, without any regard to that of ours....

The third objection to the tariff is, that it will diminish our navigation. This great interest deserves every encouragement, consistent with the paramount interest of agriculture. In the order of nature it is secondary to both agriculture and manufactures. Its business is the transportation of the productions of those two superior branches of industry. It cannot, therefore, be expected that they shall be molded or sacrificed to suit its purposes; but on the contrary, navigation must accommodate itself to the actual state of agriculture and manufacturers. If, as I believe, we have nearly reached the maximum in value of our exports of raw produce to Europe, the effect hereafter will be, as it respects that branch of our trade, if we persevere in the foreign system, to retain our navigation at the point which it has now reached.... But, if I am mistaken in these views, and it should experience any reduction, the increase in our coasting tonnage resulting from the greater activity of domestic exchanges will more than compensate the injury....

According to the opponents of the domestic policy, the proposed system will force capital and labor into new and reluctant employments; we are not prepared, in consequence of the high price of wages, for the successful establishment of manufactures, and we must fail in the experiment. We have seen that the existing occupations of our society, those of agriculture, commerce, navigation, and the learned professions, are overflowing with competitors, and that the want of employment is severely felt. Now what does this bill propose? To open a new and extensive field of business in which all that choose may enter. There is no compulsion upon anyone to engage in it. An option only is given to industry to continue in the present unprofitable pursuits, or to embark in a new and promising one. The effect will be to lessen the competition in the old branches of business and to multiply our resources for increasing our comforts and augmenting the national wealth....

It is said that wherever there is a concurrence of favorable circumstances manufactures will arise of themselves, without protection; and that we should not disturb the natural progress of industry, but leave things to themselves.... Now, I contend that this proposition is refuted by all experience, ancient and modern, and in every country. If I am asked why unprotected industry should not succeed in a struggle with protected industry, I answer, the *fact* has ever been so, and that is sufficient; I reply that *uniform experience* evinces that it cannot succeed in such an unequal contest, and that is sufficient....

The next objection of the honorable gentleman from Virginia which I shall briefly notice is that the manufacturing system is adverse to the genius of our government in its tendency to the accumulation of large capitals in a few hands; in the corruption of the public morals, which is alleged to be incident to it; and in the consequent danger to the public liberty.... The greatest danger to public liberty is from idleness and vice. If manufacturers form cities, so does commerce. And the disorders and violence which proceed from the contagion of the passions are as frequent in one description of those communities as in the other.

There is no doubt but that the yeomanry of a country is the safest depository of public liberty. In all time to come, and under any probable direction of the labor of our population, the agricultural class must be much the most numerous and powerful, and will ever retain, as it ought to retain, a preponderating influence in our councils. The extent and the fertility of our lands constitute an adequate security against an excess in manufactures, and also against oppression, on the part of capitalists, toward the laboring portions of the community....

Mr. Chairman, our Confederacy comprehends, within its vast limits, great diversity of interests: agricultural, planting, farming, commercial, navigating, fishing, manufacturing. No one of these interests is felt in the same degree and cherished with the same solicitude throughout all parts of the Union. Some of them are peculiar to particular sections of our common country. But all these great interests are confided to the protection of one government — to the fate of one ship — and a most gallant ship it is, with a noble crew. If we prosper and are happy, protection must be extended to all; it is due to all....

If the promotion of those interests would not injuriously affect any other section, then everything should be done for them which would be done if it formed a distinct government. If they come into absolute collision with the interests of another section, a reconciliation, if possible, should be attempted, by mutual concession, so as to avoid a sacrifice of the prosperity of either to that of the other. In such a case, all should not be done for one which would be done, if it were separated and independent, but something; and, in devising the measure, the good of each part and of the whole should be carefully consulted. This is the only mode by which we can preserve, in full vigor, the harmony of the whole Union.

DAVY CROCKETT: A TOUR OF THE LOWELL MILLS (1835)

An Account of Col. Crockett's Tour to the North and Down East, etc., etc., Philadelphia, 1835, pp. 91–99.

Next morning I rose early and started for Lowell in a fine carriage with three gentlemen who had agreed to accompany me. I had heard so much of this place that I longed to see it; not because I had heard of the "mile of gals"; no, I left that for the gallantry of the President who is admitted, on that score, to be abler than myself; but I wanted to see the power of machinery, wielded by the keenest calculations of human skill; I wanted to see how it was that these Northerners could buy cotton, and carry it home, manufacture it, bring it back, and sell it for half nothing; and in the meantime, be well to live, and make money besides.

We stopped at the large stone house at the head of the falls of the Merrimac River, and having taken a little refreshment, went down among the factories. The dinner bells were ringing, and the folks pouring out of the houses like bees out of a gum. I looked at them as they passed, all well dressed, lively, and genteel in their appearance; indeed, the girls looked as if they were coming from a quilting frolic. We took a turn round, and after dining on a fine salmon, again returned, and entered the factories.

The outdoor appearance was fully sustained by the whole of the persons employed in the different rooms. I went in among the young girls, and talked with many of them. Not one expressed herself as tired of her employment, or oppressed with work; all talked well, and looked healthy. Some of them were very handsome; and I could not help observing that they kept the prettiest inside, and put the homely ones on the outside rows.

I could not help reflecting on the difference of conditions between these females, thus employed, and those of other populous countries, where the female character is degraded to abject slavery. Here were thousands, useful to others, and enjoying all the blessings of freedom, with the prospect before them of future comfort and respectability; and however we, who only hear of them, may call their houses workshops and prisons, I assure my neighbors there is every enjoyment of life realized by these persons, and there can be but few who are not happy. It cannot be otherwise; respectability depends upon being neighborlike; here everybody works, and therefore no one is degraded by it; on the contrary, those who don't work are not estimated.

There are more than 5,000 females employed in Lowell; and when you come to see the amount of labor performed by them, in superintending the different machinery, you will be astonished.

Twelve years ago, the place where Lowell now rises in all its pride was a sheep pasture. It took its name from Francis C. Lowell, the projector of its manufactories, and was incorporated in 1826 — then a mere village. The fall, obtained by a canal from the Merrimac River, is thirty-two feet, affording two levels for mills, of thirteen and seventeen feet; and the whole water of the river can be used.

There are about 14,000 inhabitants. It contains nine meetinghouses; appropriates $7,500 for free schools; provides instruction for 1,200 scholars, daily; and about 3,000 annually partake of its benefits. It communicates with Boston by the Middlesex Canal (the first ever made in the United States); and in a short time the railroad to Boston will be completed, affording every facility of intercourse to the seaboard.

This place has grown by, and must depend on, its manufactures. Its location renders it important, not only to the owners but to the nation. Its consumption not only employs the thousands of its own population but many thousands far away from them. It is calculated not only to give individual happiness and prosperity but to add to our national wealth and independence; and instead of depending on foreign countries, to have our own materials worked up in our own country.

Some of the girls attended three looms; and they make from $1.75 to $3 per week, after paying their board. These looms weave 55 yards per day; so that one person makes 165 yards per day. Everything moves on like clockwork, in all the variety of employments; and the whole manufacture appears to be of the very best.

The owner of one of these mills, Mr. Lawrence, presented me with a suit of broadcloth, made out of wool bought from Mark Cockral, of Mississippi, who sold them about 4,000 pounds, and it was as good cloth as the best I ever bought for best imported.

The calico made here is beautiful, and of every variety of figure and color. To attempt to give a description of the manner in which it is stamped and colored is far beyond my abilities. One thing I must state, that after the web is wove, and before they go further, it is actually passed over *a red-hot cylinder*, to scorch off the furze. The number of different operations is truly astonishing; and if one of my country women had the whole of the persons in her train that helped to make her gown, she would be like a captain on a field muster; and yet, when you come to look at the cost, it would take a trunk full of them to find these same people in living for one day.

I never witnessed such a combination of industry, and perhaps never will again. I saw the whole process, from the time they put in the raw material until it came out completely finished. In fact, it almost came up to the old story of a fellow walking into a patent machine with a bundle of wool under his arm, and coming out at the other end with a new coat on.

Nothing can be more agreeable than the attention that is paid by everyone connected with these establishments. Nothing appears to be kept secret; every process is shown, and with great cheerfulness. I regret that more of our Southern and Western men do not go there, as it would help much to do away with their prejudices against these manufactories....

I met the young gentlemen of Lowell, by their particular request, at supper. About one hundred sat down. Everything was in grand order and went off well. They toasted *me*, and I enlightened *them* by a speech as good as I could make; and, indeed, I considered them a good set of fellows, and as well worth speaking to as any ones I had met with. The old saying, "them that don't work should not eat," don't apply to them, for they are the "rale workies," and know how to act genteel, too; for, I assure you, I was not more kindly, and hospitably, and liberally treated anywhere than just by these same people.

JAMES RUSSELL LOWELL: OPPOSITION TO NATIONALISM IN LITERATURE (1843)

The Pioneer, January 1843.

Dr. John North, a man of some mark in his day, wrote on the first leaf of his notebook these significant words: "I beshrew his heart that gathers my opinion from anything wrote here!"

As we seated ourselves to the hard task of writing an introduction for our new literary journal, this sentence arose to our minds. It seemed to us to point clearly at the archwant of our periodical literature. We find opinions enough and to spare, but scarce any of the healthy, natural growth of our soil. If native, they are seldom more than scions of a public opinion, too often planted and watered by the prejudices or ignorant judgments of individuals, to be better than a upas tree shedding a poisonous blight on any literature that may chance to grow up under it. Or, if foreign, they are, to borrow a musical term, "recollections" of Blackwood or the quarterlies of Wilson, Macaulay, or Carlyle — not direct imitations but endeavors, as it were, to write with their cast-off pens, fresh-nibbed for cisatlantic service. The whole regiment comes one by one to our feast of letters in the same yellow domino.

Criticism, instead of being governed as it should be by the eternal and unchanging laws of beauty, which are a part of the soul's divine nature, seems rather to be a striving to reduce art to one dead level of conventional mediocrity — which only does not offend taste because it lacks even the life and strength to produce any decided impression whatever.

We are the farthest from wishing to see what many so ardently pray for; namely, a *national* literature; for the same mighty lyre of the human heart answers the touch of the master in all ages and in every clime; and any literature, as far as it is national, is diseased, inasmuch as it appeals to some climatic peculiarity rather than to the universal nature. Moreover, everything that tends to encourage the sentiment of *caste*, to widen the boundary between races and so to put farther off the hope of one great brotherhood, should be steadily resisted by all good men.

But we do long for a *natural* literature. One green leaf, though of the veriest weed, is worth all the crape and wire flowers of the daintiest Paris milliners. For it is the glory of nature that in her least part she gives us all, and in that simple love token of hers we may behold the type of all her sublime mysteries; as in the least fragment of the true artist we discern the working of the same forces which culminate gloriously in a Hamlet or a Faust. We would no longer see the spirit of our people held up as a mirror to the Old World; but rather lying like one of our own inland oceans, reflecting not only the mountain and the rock, the forest and the red man, but also the steamboat and the railcar, the cornfield and the factory.

Let us learn that romance is not married to the past, that it is not the birthright of ferocious ignorance and chivalric barbarity, but that it ever was and is an inward quality, the darling child of the sweetest refinements and most gracious amenities of peaceful gentleness; and that it can never die till only water runs in these red rivers of the heart, that cunning adept which can make vague cathedrals with blazing oriels and streaming spires out of our square meeting boxes

Whose rafters sprout upon the shady side.

We do not mean to say that our writers should not profit by the results of those who have gone before them, nor gather from all countries those excellencies which are the effects of detached portions of that universal tendency to the beautiful which must be centered in the Great Artist. But let us not go forth to them; rather let us draw them by sympathy of nature to our own heart, which is the only living principle of every true work. The artist must use the tools of others and understand their use, else were their lives fruitless to him, and his, in turn, vain to all who came after; but the skill must be of his own toilsome winning, and he must not, like Goethe's magician's apprentice, let the tools become his masters.

But it seems the law of our literature to receive its impulses from without rather than from within. We ask oftener than the wise king of Ashantee, "What is thought of us in England?" We write with the fear of the newspapers before our eyes, every one of which has its critic, the Choragus of his little circle, self-elected expounder of the laws of nature—which he at first blush understands more thoroughly than they whom nature herself has chosen—and who have studied them lifelong and who unites at pleasure the executive with the judiciary to crush some offender mad enough to think for himself. Men seem endowed with an insane alacrity to believe that wisdom elects the dullest heads for her confidants, and crowd to burn incense to the hooting owl, while the thoughtful silence of the goddess makes them to mistake her for her bird.

We boast much of our freedom, but they who boast thereof the loudest have mostly a secret sense of fetters.

License they mean when they cry liberty, and there is among us too much freedom to speak and think ill—a freedom matched with which the lowest of all other slaveries were as the blue tent of heaven to a dungeon—and too little freedom to think, and speak, and act the highest and holiest promptings of the eternal soul. We cheat tomorrow to satisfy the petty dunning of today; we bribe ourselves with a bubble reputation, whose empty lightness alone lends it a momentary elevation, and show men our meanest part, as if we could make ourselves base enough to believe that we should offend their vanity by showing our noblest and highest.

Are prejudices to be overcome by groveling to them? Is truth any longer worthy of the name, when she stoops to take falsehood by the hand, and caresses her, and would fain wheedle her to forgo her proper nature? Can we make men noble, the aim and end of every literature worthy of the name, by showing them our own want of nobleness? In the name of all holy and beautiful things at once, no! We want a manly, straightforward, *true* literature, a criticism which shall give more grace to beauty and more depth to truth, by lovingly embracing them wherever they may lie hidden, and a creed whose truth and nobleness shall be ensured by its being a freedom from all creeds.

The young heart of every generation looks forth upon the world with restless and bitter longing. To it the earth still glitters with the dews of a yet unforfeited Eden, and in the midst stands the untasted tree of knowledge of good and evil. We hear men speak of the restless spirit of the age, as if our day were peculiar in this regard. But it has always been the same. The young is radical, the old, conservative; they who have not, struggle to get, and they who have gotten, clench their fingers to keep. The young, exulting in its tight and springy muscles, stretches out its arms to clasp the world as its plaything; and the old bids it be a good boy and mind its papa, and it shall have sugar plums.

But still the new spirit yearns and struggles, and expects great things; still the old shakes its head, ominous of universal anarchy; still the world rolls calmly on, and the youth grown old shakes its wise head at the next era. Is there any more danger to be looked for in the radicalism of youth than in the conservatism of age? Both gases must be mixed ere the cooling rain will fall on our seedfield.

The true reason for the fear which we often see expressed of a freedom which shall be debased into destructiveness and license is to be found in a false judgment of the natural progress of things. Cheerfully will men reverence all that is *true*, whether in the new or the old. It is only when you would force them to revere falsehoods that they will reluctantly throw off all reverence, without which the spirit of man must languish and at last utterly die. Truth, in her natural and infinitely various exponents of beauty and love, is all that the soul reverences long; and, as truth is universal and absolute, there can never be any balance in the progress of the soul till one law is acknowledged in all her departments.

Radicalism has only gone too far when it has *hated* conservatism, and has despised all reverence because conservatism is based upon it, forgetting that it is only so inasmuch as it is a needful part of nature. To have claimed that reverence

should not play at blind-man's-buff had been enough.

In this country, where freedom of thought does not shiver at the cold shadow of Spielberg (unless we name this prison of "public opinion" so), there is no danger to be apprehended from an excess of it. It is only where there is no freedom that anarchy is to be dreaded. The mere sense of freedom is of too pure and holy a nature to consist with injustice and wrong. We would fain have our journal, in some sort at least, a journal of progress, one that shall keep pace with the spirit of the age, and sometimes go near its deeper heart. Yet, while we shall aim at the gravity which is becoming of a manly literature, we shall hope also to satisfy that lighter and sprightlier element of the soul, without whose due culture the character is liable to degenerate into a morose bigotry and selfish precisianism.

To be one exponent of a young spirit which shall aim at power through gentleness, the only mean for its secure attainment, and in which freedom shall be attempered to love by a reverence for all beauty wherever it may exist, is our humble hope. And to this end we ask the help of all who feel any sympathy in such an undertaking. We are too well aware of the thousand difficulties which lie in the way of such an attempt, and of the universal failure to make what is written come near the standard of what is thought and hoped, to think that we shall not at first disappoint the expectations of our friends.

But we shall do our best, and they must bear with us, knowing that what is written from month to month can hardly have that care and study which is needful to the highest excellence, and believing that

> We shall be willing, if not apt to
>   learn;
> Age and experience will adorn
>   our mind
> With larger knowledge: and, if we
>   have done
> A wilful fault, think us not past
>   all hope,
> For once.

JOHN HUMPHREY NOYES: THE NASHOBA COMMUNITY (1828)

History of American Socialisms, John Humphrey Noyes, Philadelphia, 1870, pp. 66–72.

This experiment was made in Shelby County, Tennessee, by the celebrated Frances Wright. The objects were to form a community in which the Negro slave should be educated and upraised to a level with the whites and thus prepared for freedom; and to set an example which, if carried out, would eventually abolish slavery in the Southern states; also to make a home for good and great men and women of all countries who might there sympathize with each other in their love and labor for humanity. She invited congenial minds from every quarter of the globe to unite with her in the search for truth and the pursuit of rational happiness. Herself a native of Scotland, she became imbued with these philanthropic views through a knowledge of the sufferings of a great portion of mankind in many countries, and of the condition of the Negro in the United States in particular.

She traveled extensively in the Southern states and explained her views to many of the planters. It was during these travels that she visited the German settlement of Rappites at Harmony, on the Wabash River, and after examining the wonderful industry of that community, she was struck with the appropriateness of their system of cooperation to the carrying out of her aspirations. She also visited some of the Shaker establishments then existing in the United States, but she thought unfavorably of them. She renewed her visits to the Rappites and was present on the occasion of their removal from Harmony to Economy on the Ohio, where she continued her acquaintance with them, receiving valuable knowledge from their experience and, as it were, witnessing a new village, with its fields, orchards, gardens, vineyards, flouring mills and manufactories, rise out of the earth beneath the hands of some 800 trained laborers....

In the autumn of 1825 [when New Harmony was under full sail in the absence of Mr. Owen], Frances Wright purchased 2,000 acres of good and pleasant woodland, lying on both sides of the Wolf River in west Tennessee, about thirteen miles above Memphis. She then purchased several Negro families, comprising fifteen able hands, and commenced her practical experiment....

We are informed that Frances Wright found in her new occupation intense and ever increasing interest. But ere long she was seized by severe and reiterated sickness, which compeled her to make a voyage to Europe for the recovery of her health. "During her absence," says her biographer, "an intriguing individual has disorganized everything on the estate, and effected the removal of persons of confidence. All her serious difficulties proceeded from her white assistants, and not from the blacks."

In December of the following year [1826] she made over the Nashoba estate to a board of trustees, by a deed commencing thus:

I, Frances Wright, do give the lands after specified to General Lafayette, William Maclure, Robert Owen, Cadwallader Colden, Richardson Whitby, Robert Jennings, Robert Dale Owen, George Flower, Camilla Wright, and James Richardson, to be held by them and their associates and their successors in perpetual trust for the benefit of the Negro race.

By another deed she gave the slaves of Nashoba to the aforementioned trustees; and by still another she gave all her personal property.

In her appeal to the public in connection with this transfer, she explains at length her views of reform and her reasons for choosing the above-named trustees instead of the emancipation or colonization societies; and in respect to education says: "No difference will be made in the schools between the white children and the children of color, whether in education or any other advantage." After further explanation of her plans she goes on to say:

It will be seen that this establishment is founded on the principle of community of property and labor: presenting every advantage to those desirous not of accumulating money but of enjoying life and rendering services to their fellow creatures; these fellow creatures, that is, the blacks here admitted, requiting these services by services equal or greater, by filling occupations which their habits render easy, and which, to their guides and assistants, might be difficult or unpleasing.

No life of idleness, however, is proposed to the whites. Those who cannot work must give an equivalent in property. Gardening or other cultivation of the soil, useful trades practised in the society or taught in the school, the teaching of every branch of knowledge, tending the children, and nursing the sick will present a choice of employment sufficiently extensive....

In March 1828, the trustees published a communication in the *Nashoba Gazette* explaining the difficulties they had to contend with and the causes why the experience of two years had modified the original plan of Frances Wright. They show the impossibility of a cooperative community succeeding without the members composing it are superior beings; "for," say they, "if there be introduced into such a society thoughts of evil and unkindness, feelings of intolerance and words of dissension, it cannot prosper. That which produces in the world only commonplace jealousies and everyday squabbles is sufficient to destroy a community."

The society had admitted some members to labor, and others as boarders from whom no labor was required; and in this they confess their error, and now propose to admit those only who possess the funds for their support.

The trustees go on to say that "they desire to express distinctly that they have deferred, for the present, the attempt to form a society of cooperative labor; and they claim for the association only the title of a Preliminary Social Community."

After describing the moral qualifications of members, who may be admitted without regard to color, they propose that each one shall yearly throw $100 into the common fund for board alone, to be paid quarterly in advance. Each one was also to build for himself or herself a small brick house, with a piazza, according to a regular plan and upon a spot of ground selected for the purpose, near the center of the lands of Nashoba....

It is probable that success did not further attend the experiment, for

Frances Wright abandoned it soon after, and in June following removed to New Harmony, where, in conjunction with William Owen, she assumed for a short time the management of the *New Harmony Gazette*, which then had its name altered to the *New Harmony and Nashoba Gazette or Free Enquirer*.

Her biographer says that she abandoned, though not without a struggle, the peaceful shades of Nashoba, leaving the property in the charge of an individual who was to hold the Negroes ready for removal to Haiti the year following. In relinquishing her experiment in favor of the race, she held herself equally pledged to the colored families under her charge, to the Southern state in which she had been a resident citizen, and to the American community at large, to remove her dependents to a country free to their color. This she executed a year after.

CATHARINE BEECHER: THE PROFESSION OF A WOMAN (1829)

Suggestions Respecting Improvements in Education, Hartford, 1829, pp. 7–16.

It is to mothers and to teachers that the world is to look for the character which is to be enstamped on each succeeding generation, for it is to them that the great business of education is almost exclusively committed. And will it not appear by examination that neither mothers nor teachers have ever been properly educated for their profession? What is the *profession of a woman*? Is it not to form immortal minds, and to watch, to nurse, and to rear the bodily system, so fearfully and wonderfully made, and upon the order and regulation of which the health and well-being of the mind so greatly depends?

But let most of our sex, upon whom these arduous duties devolve, be asked: Have you ever devoted any time and study, in the course of your education, to any preparation for these duties? Have you been taught anything of the structure, the nature, and the laws of the body which you inhabit? Were you ever taught to understand the operation of diet, air, exercise, and modes of dress upon the human frame? Have the causes which are continually operating to prevent good health and the modes by which it might be perfected and preserved ever been made the subject of any *instruction*? Perhaps almost every voice would respond, no. We have attended to almost everything more than to this; we have been taught more concerning the structure of the earth, the laws of the heavenly bodies, the habits and formation of plants, the philosophy of languages—more of *almost anything* than the structure of the human frame and the laws of health and reason.

But is it not the business, the *profession* of a woman to guard the health and form the physical habits of the young? And is not the cradle of infancy and the chamber of sickness sacred to woman alone? And ought she not to know at least some of the *general principles* of that perfect and wonderful piece of mechanism committed to her preservation and care?

The *restoration* of health is the physician's profession, but the *preservation* of it falls to other hands, and it is believed that the time will come when woman will be taught to understand something respecting the construction of the human frame; the physical results which will naturally follow from restricted exercise, unhealthy modes of dress, improper diet, and many other causes which are continually operating to destroy the health and life of the young.

Again let our sex be asked respecting the instruction they have received in the course of their education on that still more arduous and difficult department of their profession which relates to the *intellect* and the *moral susceptibilities*. Have you been taught the powers and faculties of the human mind, and the laws by which it is regulated? Have you studied how to direct its several faculties; how to restore those that are overgrown, and strengthen and mature those that are deficient? Have you been taught the best modes of *communicating* knowledge as well as of *acquiring* it? Have you learned the best mode of correcting bad *moral* habits and forming good ones? Have you made it an object to find how a selfish disposition may be made generous; how a reserved temper may be made open and frank; how pettishness and ill humor may be changed to cheerfulness and kindness? Has any woman studied her profession in this respect?

It is feared the same answer must be returned, if not from all, at least from most of our sex. No; we have acquired wisdom from the observation and experience of others on almost *all other* subjects, but the philosophy of the direction and control of the human mind has not been an object of thought or study. And thus it appears that, though it is woman's *express business* to rear the body and form the mind, there is scarcely anything to which her attention has been less directed.

But this strange and irrational neglect, may be considered as the result, of an equal neglect as it respects those whose *exclusive* business it is, to form the mind and communicate knowledge. To the parents of a family there are many other cares committed besides the formation of the mental and moral habits of children. Indeed, the pecuniary circumstances of most parents will allow them to devote but little time to the discharge of such duties....

Another defect in education is that it has not been made a *definite object* with teachers *to prepare their pupils to instruct others*. For of how comparatively little value is knowledge laid up in the mind if it is never to be imparted to others, and yet how few have ever been taught to communicate their ideas with facility and propriety. That there is a best way of *teaching* as well as of doing everything else cannot be disputed, and this can no more be learned by *intuition* than can any of the mechanical arts. This can be made an object of instruction as much as any other art, and a woman, ordinarily, might be *taught* to converse with ease and fluency, and to communicate knowledge with accuracy and perspicuity, with far less time and effort than is now given to the acquisition of *music*.

If a teacher, in communicating ideas, should make it a part of the *duty* of a scholar to communicate the same to a third person, either to a child already ignorant or to some friend who would give a listening ear, much would be accomplished in this way. During many recitations it is desirable to induce the pupils to ask questions and express opinions with this object in view. Nothing aids more in this art than attempting to *teach others*, and all who become teachers will probably find that in this and various other ways they *receive* almost as much benefit as they *confer*.

If all females were not only well educated themselves but were prepared to communicate in an easy manner their stores of knowledge to others; if they not only knew how to regulate their own minds, tempers, and habits but how to effect improvements in those around them, the face of society would speedily be changed. The time *may* come when the world will look back with wonder to behold how much time and effort have been given to the mere cultivation of the memory, and how little mankind have been aware of what every teacher, parent, and friend could accomplish in forming the social, intellectual, and moral character of those by whom they are surrounded.

THOMAS SKIDMORE: THE UNEQUAL DISTRIBUTION OF PROPERTY (1829)

The Rights of Man to Property!, New York, 1829, pp. 355–390.

If a man were to ask me to what I would compare the unequal distribution of property which prevails in the world, and has ever prevailed, I would say that it reminds me of a large party of gentlemen who should have a common right to dine at one and the same public table; a part of whom should arrive first, sit down and eat what they chose, and, then, because the remaining part came later to dinner, should undertake to monopolize the whole and deprive them of the opportunity of satisfying their hunger, but upon terms such as those who had feasted should be pleased to prescribe.

Such, now, is the actual condition of the whole human race. Those who have gone before us have been the first to sit down to the table and to enjoy themselves without interruption from those who came afterward; and, not content with this enjoyment, they have disposed of the whole dinner in such a manner that nine-tenths of the beings that now people this globe have not wherewith to dine, but upon terms such as these first monopolizers, or those to whom they pretend they have conferred their own power as successors, shall choose to dictate. It is as if, after dining till they were satisfied, a general scramble ensued for what remained on the table; and those who succeeded in filling their pockets and other receptacles with provisions should have something to give to their children; but those who should have the misfortune to get none, or having got it, should lose it again, through fraud, calamity, or force, should have none for theirs, to the latest generation....

Three hundred thousand freemen in this state hold votes in their hands, which no power that you can command can take out; and of these freemen, more than 250,000 are men whom a preceding generation, together with yourselves and their own ignorance of their rights, have conspired to place in situations such that they have no property in the state of which they are citizens; although their title to such property is as good as that of any man that breathes....

Title to property exists for all, and for all alike; not because others have been nor because they have *not* been; not because they had a certain being for a parent rather than another being; not because they appear later or earlier on the stage of life than others; not because of purchase, of conquest, of preoccupancy, or what not; *but because they are; because they exist. I am; therefore is property mine*, as much so as any man's, and that without asking any man's permission; without paying any man's price; without knowing or caring further than as my equal right extends, whether any other human being exists or not.

Such is the language of nature; such is the language of right; and such are the principles which will justify any people in pulling down any government which denies, even to a *single* individual of the human race, his possession, his real, tangible possession, of this inalienable right of nature or its unquestionable equivalent. How much more so, then, is it the duty of any such people to destroy their own government when *more than nine-tenths*, it may be, are deprived of rights which the Creator gave them when He gave them existence?...

Let the men of all nations be made equal among themselves in point of property, and then will wars be immediately self-extinguished forever. Keep up this unnatural inequality in wealth which now exists, and they will exist as long as two nations shall be found in existence.... It appears, then, that conquerors grow out of a state of unequal possession of property; and without such an unequal possession they would never have existed. It appears, also, that by destroying this inequality everywhere conquerors and warriors would be destroyed also....

In all the principles of the rights of property which are ... seen to have been almost insensibly adopted, *there is not one which has been adopted on any consideration, correct or otherwise, of its own merits.* Usage has done everything. Custom, practice, habit has made all the law; and made it at times and under circumstances in which it was of no consequence to the generation then being, whether the principles involved in the custom were good in themselves or not; whether they would be productive of immense injury or not when they should come to have a dense population to act

upon; whether they were consistent with the rigid rights of their own generation or not; whether they preserved the rights of posterity or sacrificed them with a most unsparing hand....

How ridiculously absurd must those political physicians appear who shall oppose or attempt to postpone such enjoyment of their rights by the great mass of the people until they shall receive, as the phrase is, the benefit of education. If they be sincere in their belief that such education is so very indispensable as a previous step to this enjoyment, and that the people are not now sufficiently instructed, let me ask them how, under present circumstances, is it ever possible to give it? Is a family where both parents and children are suffering daily in their animal wants, where excessive toil is required to obtain the little they enjoy, where the unkind and the unfriendly passions generated by such a wretched condition of things reign with full sway — is such a family in a situation to receive instruction?

Even if the children attend public institutions of education as punctually as may be wished, where is that equality of rank and condition as well between their parents as between themselves, which is so necessary to banish even from among children those envious remarks on dress, etc., etc., which now render our public schools in a measure abortive?

Political dreamers! Reformers, if you prefer that I should call you so! Feed first the hungry; clothe first the naked or ill-clad; provide comfortable homes for all by hewing down colossal estates among us and equalizing all property; take care that the animal wants be supplied first, that even the *apprehension* of want be banished; and then will you have a good field and good subjects for education. Then will instruction be conveyed without obstacle; for the wants, the unsatisfied wants of the body, will not interfere with it.

In the meantime, let all remember that those who undertake to *hold back* the people from their rights of property ... until education, as they call it, can first be communicated (though ... they now know more of all that is valuable among men than those who attempt to teach them), either do not understand themselves or pursue the course they *are* pursuing for the purpose of diverting the people from the possession of these rights, that they may be held in bondage even yet longer. It becomes the people to consider and reflect how far it is proper for them to *suffer* themselves to be thus *decoyed* out of the enjoyment of their rights, even for a single hour, by any such fallacious pretexts....

The truth is, all men are fitted for the enjoyment of their rights when they know what they are. And until that time they do not desire them. They languish in misery and wretchedness, every new day being a new day of sorrow to them, when they do not perceive them and seem rather disposed to charge their evil condition to some "bad luck," as they call it; to some imaginary decree of destiny; to some superstitious interference with their happiness than to any possession by others of property which belongs to *them*.

Thus is it the case with the poor and the rich passing now in review before us. The former does not imagine that it is the latter which renders his life miserable and wretched. He does not conceive that it is he who fills his cup with bitterness, and visits himself and his family with the afflictions of slavery.... In the same wandering and benighted spirit do both the poor and the rich, the proprietor and nonproprietor, he who has everything and he who has nothing cheat themselves, daily, with self-delusions.

How came this to be your property? If I ask a man such a question, he immediately replies, "I bought it of such a one." "Well, then, I suppose he had *a right to sell it* to you?" "Certainly," he answers. "How came *he* by it?" I ask next. "He purchased of such a one." "And he, I suppose, had a right to sell, too?" "Undoubtedly." And so we go on inquiring, till we come even to the days of Adam. How came *he* by it? is the next question. And the true but hurried answer is, "God gave it to him!"

Here, for the first time, reason begins to awake and see where rights originate. What! And did God give rights to Adam which He has not given to you? Did God declare to the man of His first creation that *he* not only should have the *use* of this fair paradise, as it is said to have been, free of all charge, but should also have the power to say that no human being after him should have the use of it at all, forever? For, if Adam have the power to sell, so also has he power *not to sell;* he has power to deny its use to any or to all. Better, far better, for mankind if such is a correct foundation for our right to property that Adam had never been; for then we should have possessed it, without buying of him *who never bought himself* and to whom it was never *given* for the purpose of selling to others, but for the satisfaction of his wants, so long as he should have any; that is, so long as he should live....

Thus does it appear that one generation cannot sell, give, or convey, even if it had the right, to another. The reason is that the one is dead; the other is living. The one is present; the other, absent. They do not and cannot *meet* to come to a treaty, to make delivery, to give or receive. He who is dying is present; so soon as he is dead, he is past, and is no nearer to us in an instant after life has departed, than if he had died a thousand centuries ago. Patience becomes exhausted in thus chasing away the phantoms on which possessors of property found their title to it; and on which, too, the poor yield their assent to the validity of such title. But it is useful to dispel such errors from the minds of both the one and the other; that one may not put up a claim which he shall see he cannot support; and that the other may not confirm it through a misunderstanding of its real character.

But if property thus derived does not give to its possessor title, how are debts to be founded upon it? How am I to purchase of another that which is already truly my own? How is a man truly to sell

that which does not belong to him? If it does not belong to him, in unimpeachable right, he cannot give unimpeachable title; and unless he can give such title, he cannot have any just claim to receive consideration. If he *think* he has such title, he may be very honest in his opinions; but this would not make it the better for him. Title does not come into any man's possession merely by the force of imagination. It has other origin than this. To allow a man to sell that which is not his would be to compel someone to pay for that which, in true right, is already his own, without payment at all of any kind or of any amount.

Let no man, therefore, say that another owes him and ought to pay him; let him rather first inquire into the title by which he has held that which he pretends he has sold; let him inquire first if it was his own to sell. Let him ascertain if the pretended debtor, through his ignorance of his own rights, has not been placed, by his own government, in necessitous circumstances; and that himself has, by the same government, been placed in unjust affluent circumstances. If both of these suppositions are true, then there is no debt existing between them. He who is called the debtor has only received that which belonged to him of right; and he who calls himself the creditor has only parted with that which he never had the right to possess or retain. Debts, therefore, and the same is also to be said of contracts, in the present order of society, are obligations having no moral force;

especially as between rich and poor; and so long as it exists never can have any....

Let society ... be so modified as to give to each man his original right to property, at the proper season of his life, equal to that of any other man's, together with equal, early, and ample education; and then debts will have a good moral foundation on which to rest. At present, debt is little more or less than extortion, practised upon the needy, who have not and never have had what is their own, by those who have not only their own but also what belongs to those to whom they undertake to sell. It is like the thief selling his stolen goods to the true and original owner....

What is called wealth, therefore, is nothing less than the power to make prisoners of our fellowmen; and to compel them to erect for its possessor a palace of marble, for example, when of his own equal or equivalent industry he could not erect it himself. But it is time that those who desire to be rich should desire to be so without enslaving their fellowmen. And it is altogether easier to do so without such a crying injustice than it is with it....

Under the present unequal distribution of property, where labor is the sole resource the poor have by which to maintain their existence, degraded as it is by the slavery in which they are plunged, it is not wonderful that they have been found to be opposed to the introduction of improvements. Fruitless and unavailing as such opposition is, it is yet less unreasonable than at first sight it may appear to be.... May not improvement extend to such a degree that there will be no demand for his labor? Or if it does not reach this point, will it not approach so near it as to make him an extreme sufferer? Let it not be forgotten that while, on the one hand, laborsaving machinery is advancing in its march to perfection with rapid strides and diminishing demand for labor, so, on the other, are the numbers of the poor, among whom this demand is to be shared, augmenting in a fearful ratio.

It will be said, perhaps, that by reducing price, the direct and certain consequence of improvements (otherwise they do not deserve the name), consumption is augmented; and, therefore, the demand is increased. This is true only in a limited degree; for, as these improvements supersede, sooner or later, in a great measure, all demand for the labor of the poor, it dries up their resources faster than it multiplies them; this, in the end, diminishes rather than increases the demand; and the consequence is that, as inventions, any more than revolutions, never go backward, are never given up when their benefits are once tasted; that the whole laboring population must perish, as it were, in a sort of self-destruction, like useless beings on the earth, where, it would seem, they have no right to appear; or that they must avert such a calamity by the best means in their power.

That they cannot destroy the existence, and even increase, of laborsaving machines and processes is evident from this; that every one of those whose feelings are enlisted against the inutility to them, on account of their destroying demand for their labor, whenever he has occasion, purchases, because they come cheaper, the very productions afforded by the agents which he so much deprecates. Of what use, then, is it for a laboring man to cry out against improvements when he goes and buys a coat, for example, or rather the materials of it, at a low price, which these very improvements have made? It is reward that keeps these improvements in existence; and it is not a volley of hard words and abuse that will do them any injury. If, then, the poor themselves contribute, and as they do, by an unavoidable necessity, to the support of that which threatens their own destruction, what hope have they to escape? It is not the rich, certainly, that *will; even if it were right that they should;* and we see the poor *cannot* forego the advantages, individually speaking, of these inventions. How then, are they to avert so great a calamity?

The steam engine is not injurious to the poor when they can have the benefit of it; and this, on supposition, being *always* the case, instead of being looked upon as a curse, would be hailed as a blessing. If, then, it is seen that the steam engine, for example, is likely to greatly impoverish or destroy the poor, what have they to do but to lay hold of it and make it their own? let them appropriate, also, in the same way, the cotton factories, the woolen factories, the iron foundries, the rolling mills, houses, churches, ships, goods, steamboats, fields of agriculture, etc., ... as is their right. And they will never have occasion any more to consider that as an

evil which never deserved that character; which, on the contrary, is all that is good among men; and of which we cannot, under these new circumstances, have too much. It is an equal division of property that makes all right, and an equal transmission of it to posterity keeps it so....

In fine, let the people awake to their rights; let them understand in what they consist; let them see the course they must pursue to obtain them; let them follow up that course by informing, each as many as he can, his fellow citizens of the truth which this work contains; let all cooperate in the early and effectual accomplishment of the objects it recommends; and these objects will easily and speedily be achieved and none will have labored in vain.

A PLEA FOR MANHOOD SUFFRAGE (1829)

Proceedings and Debates of the Virginia State Convention, of 1829–30, Richmond, 1830, pp. 25–31.

Your memorialists, as their designation imports, belong to that class of citizens who, not having the good fortune to possess a certain portion of land, are, for that cause only, debarred from the enjoyment of the right of suffrage....

Comprising a very large part, probably a majority, of male citizens of mature age, they have been passed by, like aliens or slaves, as if destitute of interest, or unworthy of a voice, in measures involving their future political destiny; while the free-holders, sole possessors, under the existing Constitution, of the elective franchise have, upon the strength of that possession alone, asserted and maintained in themselves the exclusive power of new-modeling the fundamental laws of the state: in other words, have seized upon the sovereign authority....

Among the doctrines inculcated in the great charter handed down to us as a declaration of the rights pertaining to the good people of Virginia and their posterity, "as the basis and foundation of government," we are taught,

That all men are by nature equally free and independent, and have certain inherent rights, of which, when they enter into a state of society, they cannot, by any compact, deprive or divest their posterity: namely, the enjoyment of life and liberty, with the means of acquiring and possessing property, and pursuing and obtaining happiness and safety.

That all power is vested in, and consequently derived from, the people.

That a majority of the community hath an indubitable, unalienable, and indefeasible right to reform, alter, or abolish the government.

That no man, nor set of men, are entitled to exclusive or separate emoluments or privileges, but in consideration of public services.

That all men, having sufficient evidence of permanent common interest with and attachment to the community have a right of

suffrage, and cannot be taxed or deprived of their property without their consent, or that of their representative, nor bound by any law to which they have not, in like manner, assented, for the public good.

How do the principles thus proclaimed accord with the existing regulation of suffrage?...

Surely it were much to be desired that every citizen should be qualified for the proper exercise of all his rights and the due performance of all his duties. But the same qualifications that entitle him to assume the management of his private affairs and to claim all other privileges of citizenship equally entitle him, in the judgment of your memorialists, to be entrusted with this, the dearest of all his privileges, the most important of all his concerns. But if otherwise, still they cannot discern in the possession of land any evidence of peculiar merit or superior title. ...

Virtue, intelligence are not among the products of the soil. Attachment to property, often a sordid sentiment, is not to be confounded with the sacred flame of patriotism. The love of country, like that of parents and offspring, is engrafted in our nature. It exists in all climates, among all classes, under every possible form of government. Riches more often impair it than poverty. Who has it not is a monster.

Your memorialists feel the difficulty of undertaking calmly to repel charges and insinuations involving in infamy themselves and so large a portion of their fellow citizens. To be deprived of their rightful equality, and to hear as an apology that they are too ignorant and vicious to enjoy it, is no ordinary trial of patience. Yet they will suppress the indignant emotions these sweeping denunciations are well calculated to excite. The freeholders themselves know them to be unfounded. Why else are arms placed in the hands of a body of disaffected citizens, so ignorant, so depraved, and so numerous?

In the hour of danger, they have drawn no invidious distinctions between the sons of Virginia. The muster rolls have undergone no scrutiny, no comparison with the land books, with a view to expunge those who have been struck from the ranks of freemen. If the landless citizens have been ignominiously driven from the polls, in time of peace, they have at least been generously summoned, in war, to the battlefield. Nor have they disobeyed the summons, or, less profusely than others, poured out their blood in the defense of that country which is asked to disown them. Will it be said they owe allegiance to the government that gives them protection?

Be it so; and if they acknowledge the obligation; if privileges are really extended to them in defense of which they may reasonably be required to shed their blood, have they not motives, irresistible motives, of attachment to the community? Have they not an interest, a deep interest, in perpetuating the blessings they enjoy, and a right, consequently, to guard those blessings, not

from foreign aggression merely but from domestic encroachment?

But, it is said, yield them this right and they will abuse it. Property, that is, landed property, will be rendered insecure, or at least overburdened by those who possess it not. The freeholders, on the contrary, can pass no law to the injury of any other class which will not more injuriously affect themselves. The alarm is sounded, too, of danger from large manufacturing institutions, where one corrupt individual may sway the corrupt votes of thousands. It were a vain task to attempt to meet all the flimsy pretexts urged, to allay all the apprehensions felt or feigned by the enemies of a just and liberal policy. The danger of abuse is a dangerous plea. Like *necessity*, the detested plea of the tyrant, or the still more detestable plea of the Jesuit, *expediency*, it serves as an everready apology for all oppression....

To deny to the great body of the people all share in the government on suspicion that they may deprive others of their property; to rob them in advance of their rights; to look to a privileged order as the fountain and depository of all power is to depart from the fundamental maxims, to destroy the chief beauty, the characteristic feature, indeed, of republican government.

Nor is the danger of abuse thereby diminished, but greatly augmented. No community can exist, no representative body be formed, in which some one division of persons or section of country, or some two or more combined, may not preponderate and oppress the rest. The East may be more powerful than the West, the lowlanders than the highlanders, the agricultural than the commercial or manufacturing classes. To give all power, or an undue share, to one is obviously not to remedy but to ensure the evil. Its safest check, its best corrective is found in a general admission of all upon a footing of equality. So intimately are the interests of each class in society blended and interwoven, so indispensible is justice to all, that oppression in that case becomes less probable from any one, however powerful. Nor is this mere speculation....

What security ... is there against the injustice of the freeholders? How is the assertion made good that they can pass no law affecting the rights of others without more injuriously affecting their own? They cannot do this, it is said, because they possess, in common with other citizens, all personal rights, and, in addition, the rights pertaining to their peculiar property. And if this be a satisfactory reason, then one landholder in each county or district would suffice to elect the representative body; or, the impossibility of injuring others being shown, a single landholder in the commonwealth might still more conveniently exercise the sovereign power.

But, is not the proposition obviously false? What is there to prevent their imposing upon others undue burdens, and conferring on themselves unjust exemptions? Supplying the public exigencies by a capitation or other tax exclusively or oppressively operating on the other portions of the community? Exacting from the latter, in common with slaves, menial services? Placing around their own persons and property more efficient guards? Providing for their own injuries speedier remedies? Denying to the children of all other classes admission to the public seminaries of learning? Interdicting to all but their own order, indeed, the power to elect, and the right to be elected, are most intimately if not inseparably united; all offices of honor or emolument, civil or military? Why can they not do all this, and more? Where is the impossibility? It would be unjust: admirable logic! Injustice can be predicated only of nonfreeholders.

Still, it is said the nonfreeholders have no just cause of complaint. A freehold is easily acquired. The right of suffrage, moreover, is not a natural right. Society may grant, modify, or withhold it as expediency may require. Indeed, all agree that certain regulations are proper; those, for example, relating to age, sex, and citizenship. At best, it is an idle contest for an abstract right whose loss is attended with no practical evil.

If a freehold be, as supposed, so easily acquired, it would seem highly impolitic, to say no more, to insist on retaining an odious regulation, calculated to produce no other effect than to excite discontent. But the fact is not so. The thousands expelled from the polls too well attest the severity of its operation. It is by no means easy or convenient for persons whom fortune or inclination have engaged in other than agricultural pursuits to withdraw from those pursuits, or from the support of their families, the amount requisite for the purchase of a freehold. To compel them to do this, to vest that sum in unproductive property, is to subject them, over and above the original cost, the assessments upon it, and the probable loss by deterioration, to an annual tax, equivalent to the profits they might have derived from the capital thus unprofitably expended.

What would be thought of a tax imposed, or penalty inflicted, upon all voters for exercising what should be the unbought privilege of every citizen? How much more odious is the law that imposes this tax, or rather, it may be said, inflicts this penalty, on one portion of the community, probably the larger and least able to encounter it, and exempts the other?

The right of suffrage, however, it seems, is not a natural right. If by natural is meant what is just and reasonable, then nothing is more reasonable than that those whose purses contribute to maintain, whose lives are pledged to defend the country, should participate in all the privileges of citizenship. But say it is not a natural right. Whence did the freeholders derive it? How become its exclusive possessors? Will they arrogantly tell us they own the country because they hold the land? The right by which they hold the land is not itself a natural right, and, by consequence, nothing claimed as incidental to it….

Let us concede that the right of suffrage is a social right; that it must of necessity be regulated by society. Still the question recurs, is the existing limitation proper? For obvious reasons, by almost universal consent, women and children, aliens and slaves are excluded. It were useless to discuss the propriety of a rule that scarcely admits of diversity of opinion. What is concurred in by those who constitute the society, the body politic, must be taken to be right. But the exclusion of these classes, for reasons peculiarly applicable to them, is no argument for excluding others to whom no one of those reasons applies.

It is said to be *expedient*, however, to exclude nonfreeholders also. Who shall judge of this expediency? The society. And does that embrace the proprietors of certain portions of land only? Expedient, for whom? For the freeholders. A harsh appelation would he deserve who, on the plea of expediency, should take from another his property. What, then, should be said of him who, on that plea, takes from another his rights, upon which the security, not of his property only but of his life and liberty depends?

But the nonfreeholders are condemned for pursuing an abstract right, whose privation occasions no practical injury.…

Never can your memorialists agree that pecuniary burdens or personal violence are the sole injuries of which men may dare to complain. It may be that the freeholders have shown no disposition greatly to abuse the power they have assumed. They may have borne themselves with exemplary moderation; but their unrepresented brethren cannot submit to a degrading regulation which takes from them, on the supposition of mental inferiority or moral depravity, all share in the government under which they live. They cannot yield to pretensions of political superiority founded on the possession of a bit of land, of whatever dimensions. They cannot acquiesce in political bondage, because those who affect to sway over them the rod of empire treat them leniently. The privilege which they claim, they respectfully insist, is theirs as of right; and they are under no obligation to assign any reason whatever for claiming it but that it is their own.

Let the picture be for a moment reversed. Let it be imagined that the nonfreeholders, possessing the physical superiority which alone can cause their political influence to be dreaded, should at some future day, *after the manner of the freeholders*, take the government into their own hands and deal out to the latter the same measure of justice they have received at their hands. It is needless to inquire into the equity of such a proceeding; but would they not find for it in the example set them at least a plausible excuse, and to the freeholders' remonstrance retort the freeholders' argument? That argument your memorialists will not now recapitulate; they leave it to others to make the application.

MRS. SAMUEL HARRISON SMITH: THE INAUGURATION OF ANDREW JACKSON (1829)

The First Forty Years of Washington Society, Gaillard Hunt, ed., New York, 1906, pp. 290–298.

It [the inauguration] … was not a thing of detail or a succession of small incidents. No, it was one grand whole, an imposing and majestic spectacle, and, to a reflective mind, one of moral sublimity. Thousands and thousands of people, without distinction of rank, collected in an immense mass round the Capitol, silent, orderly, and tranquil, with their eyes fixed on the front of that edifice, waiting the appearance of the President in the portico. The door from the rotunda opens; preceded by the marshals, surrounded by the judges of the Supreme Court, the old man with his gray locks, that crown of glory, advances, bows to the people who greet him with a shout that rends the air. The cannons from the heights around, from Alexandria and Fort Warburton, proclaim the oath he has taken and all the hills reverberate the sound. It was grand; it was sublime! An almost breathless silence succeeded, and the multitude was still, listening to catch the sound of his voice, though it was so low as to be heard only by those nearest to him.

After reading his speech; the oath was administered to him by the chief justice. Then Marshall presented the Bible. The President took it from his hands, pressed his lips to it, laid it reverently down, then bowed again to the people — yes, to the people in all their majesty. And had the spectacle closed here, even Europeans must have acknowledged that a free people, collected in their might, silent, and tranquil, restrained solely by a moral power, without a shadow around of military force, was majesty rising to sublimity and far surpassing the majesty of kings and princes surrounded with armies and glittering in gold.

But I will not anticipate, but will give you an account of the inauguration in mere detail. The whole of the preceding day, immense crowds were coming into the city from all parts, lodgings could not be obtained, and the newcomers had to go to Georgetown, which soon overflowed, and others had to go to Alexandria. I was told the Avenue and adjoining streets were so crowded on Tuesday afternoon that it was difficult to pass.

A national salute was fired early in the morning, and ushered in March 4. By 10 o'clock, the Avenue was crowded with carriages of every description, from the splendid baronet and coach, down to wagons and carts, filled with women and children, some in finery and some in rags, for it was the people's President, and all would see him; the men all walked....

The day was ... delightful, the scene animating; so we walked backward and forward, at every turn meeting some new acquaintance and stopping to talk and shake hands.... We continued promenading here until near three, returned home unable to stand, and threw ourselves on the sofa.

Someone came and informed us the crowd before the President's house was so far lessened that they thought we might enter. This time we effected our purpose. But what a scene did we witness! The majesty of the people had disappeared, and a rabble, a mob, of boys, Negroes, women, children — scrambling, fighting, romping. What a pity, what a pity! No arrangements had been made, no police officers placed on duty, and the whole house had been inundated by the rabble mob. We came too late.

The President, after having been *literally* nearly pressed to death and almost suffocated and torn to pieces by the people in their eagerness to shake hands with Old Hickory, had retreated through the back way, or south front, and had escaped to his lodgings at Gadsby's. Cut glass and china to the amount of several thousand dollars had been broken in the struggle to get the refreshments. Punch and other articles had been carried out in tubs and buckets, but had it been in hogsheads it would have been insufficient; ice creams and cake and lemonade for 20,000 people, for it is said that number were there, though I think the estimate exaggerated. Ladies fainted, men were seen with bloody noses, and such a scene of confusion took place as is impossible to describe; those who got in could not get out by the door again but had to scramble out of windows.

At one time, the President, who had retreated and retreated until he was pressed against the wall, could only be secured by a number of gentlemen forming round him and making a kind of barrier of their own bodies; and the pressure was so great that Colonel Bomford, who was one, said that at one time he was afraid they should have been pushed down or on the President. It was then the windows were thrown open and the torrent found an outlet, which otherwise might have proved fatal.

This concourse had not been anticipated and therefore not provided against. Ladies and gentlemen only had been expected at this levee, not the people *en masse*. But it was the people's day, and the people's President, and the people would rule. God grant that one day or other the people do not put down all rule and rulers. I fear, enlightened freemen as they are, they will be found, as they have been found in all ages and countries where they get the power in their hands, that of all tyrants, they are the most ferocious, cruel, and despotic. The noisy and disorderly rabble in the President's house brought to my mind descriptions I had read of the mobs in the Tuileries and at Versailles. I expect to hear the carpets and furniture are ruined; the streets were muddy, and these guests all went thither on foot.

JOHN C. CALHOUN: STATES' RIGHTS AND NULLIFICATION (1832)

Reports and Public Letters of John C. Calhoun, Richard K. Crallé, ed., New York, 1856, Vol. VI, pp. 193–209.

We, the people of South Carolina, assembled in convention in our sovereign capacity as one of the parties to the compact which formed the Constitution of the United States, have declared the act of Congress, approved the 14th of July, 1832, to alter and amend the several acts imposing duties on imports, and the acts which it alters and amends to be unconstitutional, and therefore null and void; and have invested the legislature of the state with power to adopt such measures, not repugnant to the Constitution of the United States nor of this state, as it may deem proper to carry the same into effect. In taking this step, we feel it to be due to the intimate political relations existing between the states of the Union, to make known to them, distinctly, the principles on which we have acted, with the cause and motive by which we have been influenced, to fulfill which is the object of the present communication.

For this purpose, it will be necessary to state, summarily, what we conceive to be the nature and character of the Constitution of the United States, with the rights and duties of the states — so far as they relate to the subject — in reference both to the Union and to their own citizens; and also the character and effect, in a political point of view, of the system of protective duties contained in the acts which we have declared to be unconstitutional, as far as it may be necessary, in reference to the same subject.

We, then, hold it as unquestionable that on the separation from the Crown of Great Britain, the people of the several colonies became free and independent states, possessed of the full right of self-government; and that no power can be rightfully exercised over them but by the consent and authority of their respective states, expressed or implied. We also hold it as equally unquestionable that the Constitution of the United States is a compact between the people of the several states, constituting free, independent, and sovereign communities; that the government it created was formed and appointed to execute, according to the provisions of the instrument, the powers therein granted as the joint agent of the several states; that all its acts, transcending these powers, are simply and of themselves null and void, and that in case of such infractions, it is the right of the states, in their sovereign capacity, each acting for itself and its citizens, in like manner as they adopted the Constitution to judge thereof in the last resort and to adopt such measures — not inconsistent with the compact — as may be deemed fit to arrest the execution of the act within their respective limits. Such we hold to be the right of the states in reference to an unconstitutional act of the government; nor do we deem their duty to exercise it on proper occasions less certain and imperative than the right itself is clear.

We hold it to be a very imperfect conception of the obligation which each state contracted in ratifying the Constitution and thereby becoming a member of the Union to suppose that it would be fully and faithfully discharged simply by abstaining, on its part, from exercising the powers delegated to the government of the Union, or by sustaining it in the due execution of those powers. These are, undoubtedly, important federal duties, but there is another not less important; to resist the government, should it, under color of exercising the delegated, encroach on the reserved powers. The duty of the states is no less clear in the one case than in the other; and the obligation as binding in the one as in the other; and in like manner, the solemn obligation of an oath imposed by the states through the Constitution on all public functionaries, federal and state, to support that instrument comprehends the one as well as the other duty; as well that of maintaining the government in the due exercise of its powers as that of resisting it when it transcends them.

But the obligation of a state to resist the encroachments of the government on the reserved powers is not limited simply to the discharge of its federal duties. We hold that it embraces another, if possible, more sacred—that of protecting its citizens, derived from their original sovereign character, viewed in their separate relations. There are none of the duties of a state of higher obligation. It is, indeed, the primitive duty, preceding all others, and in its nature paramount to them all; and so essential to the existence of a state that she cannot neglect or abandon it without forfeiting all just claims to the allegiance of her citizens, and with it, her sovereignty itself. In entering into the Union, the states by no means exempted themselves from the obligation of this, the first and most sacred of their duties; nor, indeed, can they without sinking into subordinate and dependent corporations. It is true that in ratifying the Constitution they placed a large and important portion of the rights of their citizens under the joint protection of all the states, with a view to their more effectual security; but it is not less so that they reserved; at the same time, a portion still larger, and not less important, under their own immediate guardianship; and in relation to which the original obligation, to protect the rights of their citizens from whatever quarter assailed, remained unchanged and unimpaired.

Nor is it less true that the general government, created in order to preserve the rights placed under the joint protection of the states, and which, when restricted to its proper sphere, is calculated to afford them the most perfect security, may become, when not so restricted, the most dangerous enemy to the rights of their citizens, including those reserved under the immediate guardianship of the states respectively as well as those under their joint protection; and thus, the original and inherent obligation of the states to protect their citizens is united with that which they have contracted to support the Constitution, thereby rendering it the most sacred of all their duties to watch over and resist the encroachments of the government; and on the faithful performance of which we solemnly believe the duration of the Constitution and the liberty and happiness of the country depend.

But, while we hold the rights and duties of the states to be such as we have stated, we are deeply impressed with the conviction that it is due to the relation existing between them, as members of a common Union, and the respect which they ought ever to entertain toward the government ordained to carry into effect the important objects for which the Constitution was formed, that the occasion to justify a state in interposing its authority ought to be one of necessity; where all other peaceful remedies have been unsuccessfully tried; and where the only alternative is interposition on one side, or oppression of its citizens and imminent danger to the Constitution and liberty of the country on the other; and such we hold to be the present.

That the prohibitory, or protective system, which, as has been stated is embraced in the acts which we have declared to be unconstitutional, and therefore null and void, is, in fact, unconstitutional, unequal, and oppressive in its operation on this and the other staple and exporting states and dangerous to the Constitution and liberty of the country; and that (all other peaceful remedies having been tried without success) an occasion has occurred where it becomes the right and duty of the state to interpose its authority to arrest the evil within its limits, we hold to be certain; and it is under this deep and solemn conviction that we have acted.

For more than ten years the system has been the object of continued, united, and strenuous opposition on the part both of the government of the state and its representatives in Congress, and, we may add, of the other staple and exporting states.

During this long period, all the ordinary means of opposition—discussion, resolution, petition, remonstrance, and protest—have been tried and exhausted, without effect. We have, during the whole time, waited with patience under the unequal and oppressive action of the system, hoping that the final payment of the public debt, when there would be no longer a pretext for its continuance, would bring it to a termination. That period, for all practical purposes, is now passed. The small remnant of debt which now remains is amply provided for by the revenue already accrued; but the system remains in full force; its restrictive character established and openly avowed; the inequality of its action between this and other sections greatly increased; and the amount of its exertions vastly exceeding, probably doubling, the just and constitutional wants of the government.

The event which, it was hoped, would put an end to its duration has thus but served to give it increased strength; and instead of mitigating, has aggravated its most obnoxious features. Having stood this shock, it seems almost impossible that any other within the ordinary scope of events can shake it. It now stands for the first time, exclusively on its own basis, as an independent system, having a self-existing power with an unlimited capacity of increasing, which, left unopposed, must continue to expand till it controls the entire labor and capital of the staple and exporting states; subjecting them completely, as tributaries, to the great dominant and sectional interest which has grown up at their expense. With this prospect of the indefinite extent and duration of the system, we had thus presented the alternative of silently acquiescing in its oppression and danger, or of interposing as the last peaceful measure of redress the authority of the state to arrest the evil within its limits. We did not hesitate.

When we reflect on the principle on which the system rests, and from which the government claims the power to control the labor and capital of the country, and the bitter fruits it has already produced, the decay and impoverishment of an entire section of the country, and the wide spread of discord and corruption, we cannot doubt that there is involved in the issue not only the prosperity of this and the other staple and exporting states, but also the Constitution and liberty of the country. In rearing up the system it was not pretended, nor is it now, that there is in the Constitution any positive grant of power to protect manufactures; nor can it be denied that frequent attempts were made in the Convention to obtain the power, and that they all failed. And yet, without any grant and notwithstanding the failure to obtain one, it has become one of the leading powers of the government, influencing more extensively its movements and affecting more deeply and permanently the relative interests and condition of the states and the probable fate of the government itself than any or all of the enumerated powers united.

From whatever source its advocates may derive this power, whether from the right "to lay and collect taxes, duties, imposts, and excises," or from that "to regulate commerce," it plainly rests on the broad assumption that the power to impose duties may be applied, not only to effect the original objects — to raise revenue, or regulate commerce — but also to protect manufactures; and this, not as an incidental but as a substantive and independent power, without reference to revenue or commerce; and, in this character it has been used in building up the present system.

That such a power, resting on such a principle, is unauthorized by the Constitution; that it has become an instrument in the hands of the great dominant interests of the country, to oppress the weaker; that it must ultimately concentrate the whole power of the community in the general government and abolish the sovereignty of the states; and that discord, corruption, and, eventually, despotism must follow if the system be not resisted, we hold to be certain. Already we see the commencement of this disastrous train of consequences — the oppression of the weaker; the assumption by government of the right to determine, finally and conclusively, the extent of its own powers; the denial and denunciation of the right of the states to judge of their reserved powers and to defend them against the encroachments of the government, followed by discord, corruption, and the steady advance of despotic power.

That something is wrong, all admit; and that the assumption by government

of a power so extensive and dangerous, and the control which it has thereby acquired through its fiscal operations over the wealth and labor of the country, exacting, in the shape of high duties, a large portion of the annual income of our section and bestowing it in the form of monopolies and appropriations on the other, is the true cause of the existing disorder and the only adequate one that can be assigned, we cannot entertain a doubt. To this unequal and excessive fiscal action of the government may be immediately and clearly traced the growing discontent and alienation on the part of the oppressed portion of the community and the greedy pursuit of office; and with it, the increasing spirit of servility, subserviency, and corruption on the other, which all must see and acknowledge, and which every lover of the country and its institutions must deplore.

Nor is it less clear that this dangerous assumption, by which the reserved powers of the states have been transferred to the general government, is rapidly concentrating, by a necessary operation, the whole power of the government in the hands of the executive. We must be blind to the lessons of reason and experience not to see that the more a government interferes with the labor and wealth of a community, the more it exacts from one portion and bestows on another, just in the same proportion must the power of that department, which is vested with its patronage, be increased. It ought not, then, to be a subject of surprise that, with this vast increase of the power and revenues of the federal government and its unequal fiscal action, both in the collection and distribution of the latter, the power of the executive, on whose will the disposition of the patronage of the government mainly depends, and on which, in turn, depends that powerful, active, and mercenary corps of expectants, created by the morbid moneyed action of the government, should be, of late, so greatly and dangerously increased. It is indeed not difficult to see that the present state of things, if continued, must end, and that speedily, in raising this department of the government into an irresponsible and despotic power, with the capacity of perpetuating itself through its own influence; first, virtually appointing its successor, or, by controlling the presidential election, through the patronage of the government; and, finally, as the virtue and patriotism of the people decay, by the introduction and open establishment of the hereditary principle.

The federal government has, indeed, already passed through the first and most difficult part of this process, which, if permitted to proceed, must terminate, as it ever has, in the absolute and unlimited power of a single despot.

We hold it as certain that wherever the majority of a people becomes the advocate of high taxes and profuse appropriations and expenditures, there the despotic power is already, in fact, established and liberty virtually lost, be the form of government what it may; and experience has proved that the transition from this stage to the absolute power of a single individual is certain and rapid; and that it can only be arrested by the interposition of some high power out of the ordinary course. Our government has already clearly reached the first stage; and will inevitably—unless the process be arrested by some such power—speedily terminate its career in the last. In the meantime, while this train of events is consummating itself in the loss of the liberty of all, the oppression and impoverishment of this and the other staple and exporting states will necessarily advance with equal steps. The very root of the system, that from which it derives its existence and sprouts forth all its evils, is its unjust and unequal action—giving to one portion what it takes from another—and thus creating that powerful and irresistible interest in favor of high taxes and profuse expenditures, which are fast sweeping away, at the same time, the foundation of our liberty and exhausting and reducing to poverty a large portion of the community.

That such is, in truth, the real state of things, the extraordinary spectacle which our government now exhibits to the world affords the most conclusive proof. On what other principle can it be explained that a popular government, with all the forms of freedom, after having discharged a long standing and heavy public debt, should resist every effort to make a corresponding reduction of the public burden? What other cause can be assigned for a fact so remarkable as that of a free community refusing to repeal this tax, when the proceeds are, confessedly, no longer wanted, and when the embarrassment of the government is not to find the revenue but the objects on which to expend it?

Such is the nature of the disorder which the system has engendered. Of all the diseases which can afflict the body politic, we hold it to be the most inveterate and difficult to remedy. Others, originating in ignorance, delusion, or some sudden popular impulse, yield to the influence of time and reflection; and we may, accordingly, look in such cases, with confidence, for relief to the returning good sense and feelings of the community. Not so in this. Having its source in the most powerful passions of the human heart—the love of gain and power—neither time, reflection, reason, discussion, entreaty, nor remonstrance can arrest or impede its course. Nor, if left to itself, will it stop while there is a cent to be exacted or a particle of power to be acquired. With us the disease must assume the most aggravated character. There is no country in which so many and such powerful causes exist to give to the unequal fiscal action of the government, in which it originates, so powerful an impetus, and an operation so oppressive and dangerous.

When we reflect on the extent of our country, and the diversity of its interests; on the peculiar nature of the labor and production of this and the other suffering states; with how much facility they may be made subservient to the power and wealth of the other sections, as experience has shown, and how deep, radical,

and disastrous must be the change in the social and political condition of this and the other states similarly situated in reference to pursuits and population, when the increasing pressure shall reach the point at which the exactions of the government shall not leave a sufficient amount of the proceeds of labor to remunerate the expense of maintenance and supervision; we cannot but foresee, if the system be not arrested, calamity awaiting us and our posterity, greater than ever befell a free and enlightened people. Already we perceive indications of its approach that cannot be mistaken. It appears in that quarter to which, from the nature of the disease, we would naturally look for it; that quarter where labor is the least productive and is least capable of bearing the pressure of the system.

Such we hold to be the general character of the system, viewed in its political connections and its certain effects, if left to its natural operations; to arrest the evils of which, within our limits, we have interposed the authority of the state as the only peaceful remedy that remains of defending the Constitution against its encroachments, the citizens of the state against its oppression, and the liberty of the country against its corrupting influence and danger.

In performing this high and sacred duty, our anxious desire has been to embarrass the action of the government in the smallest degree possible, consistent with the object we have in view; and had it been possible to separate the portion of duties necessary for revenue from that imposed for the purpose of protection, the action of the state would have been limited exclusively to the latter. But we could have no right to discriminate when the government had made no discrimination; and if we had, it would have been impossible, as revenue and protection are so blended throughout, and the duties, as well those included in the act of July last, as those contained in the acts it alters and amends, comprehending the unprotected and the protected articles, are adjusted so obviously with the design to form one entire system of protection, as much so, as if the whole had been incorporated in a single act passed expressly with that intention, and without regard to revenue except as a mere incident.

The whole thus forming one system, equally contaminated throughout by the same unconstitutional principle, no alternative was left but to declare the entire system unconstitutional; and as such null and void. Anxious, however, while thus compelled to arrest an unconstitutional act, to continue in the discharge of all our constitutional obligations, and to bear our just and full share of the public burdens, we have, with a view to effect these objects, pledged the state to make good her proportional part of the revenue that would have accrued on the imports into the state, which may be exempted from duties, by the interposition of the state; calculated according to the rate per centum on the general imports which may, on a fair estimate, be considered requisite to meet the just and constitutional wants of the government; and have, accordingly,

authorized the government of the state to adopt the necessary measures on its part to adjust the same on the termination of the present unhappy controversy.

That so desirable an event may be speedily brought about to the satisfaction of all is our sincere desire. In taking the stand which she has, the state has been solely influenced by a conscientious sense of duty to her citizens and to the Constitution without the slightest feeling of hostility towards the interests of any section of the country, or the remotest view to revolution, or wish to terminate her connection with the Union; to which she is now, as she ever has been, devotedly attached. Her object is not to destroy, but to restore and preserve. And, in asserting her right to defend her reserved powers, she disclaims all pretension to control or interfere with the action of the government within its proper sphere, or to resume any powers that she has delegated to the government or conceded to the confederated states. She simply claims the right of exercising the powers which, in adopting the Constitution, she reserved to herself; and among them, the most important and essential of all, the right to judge, in the last resort, of the extent of her reserved powers, a right never delegated nor surrendered, nor, indeed, could be, while the state retains her sovereignty.

That it has not been, we appeal with confidence to the Constitution itself, which contains not a single grant that, on a fair construction, can be held to comprehend the power. If to this we add the fact, which the journals of the Convention abundantly establish, that reiterated but unsuccessful attempts were made, in every stage of its proceedings, to divest the states of the power in question, by conferring on the general government the right to annul such acts of the states as it might deem to be repugnant to the Constitution, and the corresponding right to coerce their obedience; we have the highest proof of which the subject is susceptible, that the power in question was not delegated, but reserved to the states. To suppose that a state, in exercising a power so unquestionable, resists the Union, would be a fundamental and dangerous error originating in a radical misconception of the nature of our political institutions. The government is neither the Union, nor its representative, except as an agent to execute its powers. The states themselves, in their confederated character, represent the authority of the Union; and, acting in the manner prescribed by the Constitution, through the concurring voice of three-fourths of their number, have the right to enlarge or diminish, at pleasure, the powers of the government, and to amend, alter, or even abolish the Constitution, and, with it, the government itself.

Correctly understood, it is not the state that interposes to arrest an unconstitutional act, but the government that passed it, which resists the authority of the Union. The government has not the right to add a particle to its powers; and to assume, on its part, the exercise of a power not granted, is plainly to oppose the confederated authority of the states, to which the right of granting powers exclusively belongs; and, in so doing, the Union itself, which they represent. On the contrary, a state, as a member of the body in which the authority of the Union resides, in arresting an unconstitutional act of the government, within its limits, so far from opposing, in reality supports the Union, and that in the only effectual mode in which it can be done in such cases. To divest the states of this right would be, in effect, to give to the government that authority over the Constitution which belongs to them exclusively; and which can only be preserved to them, by leaving to each state—as the Constitution has done—to watch over and defend its reserved powers against the encroachments of the government, and in performing which, it acts, at the same time, as a faithful and vigilant sentinel over the confederate powers of the states.

It was doubtless with these views that the Convention which framed the Constitution steadily resisted, as has been observed, the many attempts which were made, under the specious but fallacious argument of preserving the peace and harmony of the Union, to divest the states of this important right, which is not less essential to the defense of their joint confederate powers than to the preservation of their separate sovereignty and the protection of their citizens.

With these views—views on which the Convention acted in refusing to divest the states of this right—has this state acted in asserting it on the present occasion; and this with a full understanding of all the responsibilities attached to the position she has assumed, and with a determination as fixed as her conception of her right and duty is clear, to maintain it under every circumstance, and at every hazard. She has weighed all the consequences, and can see, in no possible result, greater disasters than those which must certainly follow a surrender of the right and an abandonment of her duty.

Having thus taken, immovably, her stand, there remain, to bring the controversy to a happy termination, but two possible courses. It may be effected by the government ceasing to exercise the unconstitutional power through which, under the name of duties, it has assumed the control over the labor and wealth of the country, and substituting for the present high rates an average ad valorem duty; or some other system of revenue equally just and fair; or by obtaining a positive grant of the power in the manner prescribed by the Constitution.

But, when we consider the great interests at stake and the number and magnitude of the questions involved in the issue, directly and indirectly, and the necessity of a full understanding on all the points, in order to a satisfactory and permanent adjustment of the controversy, we hold it difficult, if not impracticable, to bring it to a final and satisfactory close, short of convening again the body to whose authority and wisdom we are indebted for the Constitution. And under this conviction we have made it the duty of the legislature of the state

to apply, in the manner prescribed by the Constitution, for a general convention of the states, as the most certain, prompt, and effectual, if not the only practicable mode of terminating the conflict and restoring harmony and confidence to the country.

If the other states of the Union be actuated by the same feelings which govern us, if their desire to maintain the Constitution, to preserve the Union, and to transmit to posterity the blessings of liberty, be as strong as ours (and we doubt not that it is), this most august of all assemblies, provided by the Constitution to meet this and similar emergencies, as a great moral substitute for revolution and force, may be convened in a few months; when the present, and every other constitutional question endangering the peace and harmony of the Union may be satisfactorily adjusted.

If there be any conceivable occasion that can justify the call of a Convention of the states, we hold the present to be that occasion; and surely the framers of the Constitution, in providing a mode for calling one, contemplated that great emergencies would arise in the course of events, in which it ought to be convened. They were not so vain as to suppose that their work was so perfect as to be too clear to admit of diversity of opinion, or too strong for passion or interest to derange. They accordingly, in their wisdom, provided a double remedy to meet the contingencies, which, if not provided for might endanger our political system: one, to meet ordinary and less pressing occurrences by vesting in two-thirds of Congress the power to propose amendments to the Constitution, to be ratified by three-fourths of the states; the other, for those of a more urgent character, when some deep derangement of the system, or some great and dangerous conflict of interests or opinion, might threaten with a catastrophe the institutions of the country.

That such a remedy is provided is proof of the profound wisdom of the great men who formed our Constitution; and entitles them to the lasting gratitude of the country. But it will be in vain that their wisdom devised a remedy so admirable, a substitute so infinitely superior to the old and irrational mode of terminating such controversies as are of too high a nature to be adjusted by the force of reason, or through the ordinary tribunals, if their descendants be so blind as not to perceive its efficacy, or so intently bent on schemes of ambition and avarice as to prefer to this constitutional, peaceful, and safe remedy the wanton, hazardous, and, we may add, immoral arbitrament of force.

We hold that our country has arrived at the very point of difficulty and danger contemplated by the framers of the Constitution in providing for a General Convention of the states of the Union; and that, of course, the question now remaining to be tested is whether there be sufficient moral elevation, patriotism, and intelligence in the country to adjust, through the interposition of this highest of tribunals, whose right none can question, the conflicts which now threaten the very existence of our institutions, and liberty itself, and which, as experience has proved, there is no other body belonging to the system having sufficient weight of authority to terminate.

Such, at least, is our conviction; and we have acted accordingly. It now rests with the other states to determine whether a General Convention shall be called or not. And on that determination hangs, we solemnly believe, the future fate of the country. If it should be in favor of a call, we may, with almost perfect certainty, entertain the prospect of a speedy and happy termination of all our difficulties, followed by peace, prosperity, and lengthened political existence. But if not, we shall, by rejecting the remedy provided by the wisdom of our ancestors, prove that we deserve the fate which, in that event, will, in all probability, await the country.

THE SENECA FALLS DECLARATION ON WOMEN'S RIGHTS (1848)

History of Woman Suffrage, Elizabeth C. Stanton *et al.*, eds., New York, 1881, Vol. I, pp. 70–73.

DECLARATION OF SENTIMENTS

When, in the course of human events, it becomes necessary for one portion of the family of man to assume among the people of the earth a position different from that which they have hitherto occupied, but one to which the laws of nature and of nature's God entitle them, a decent respect to the opinions of mankind requires that they should declare the causes that impel them to such a course.

We hold these truths to be self-evident: that all men and women are created equal; that they are endowed by their Creator with certain inalienable rights; that among these are life, liberty, and the pursuit of happiness; that to secure these rights governments are instituted, deriving their just powers from the consent of the governed. Whenever any form of government becomes destructive of these ends, it is the right of those who suffer from it to refuse allegiance to it, and to insist upon the institution of a new government, laying its foundation on such principles, and organizing its powers in such form, as to them shall seem most likely to effect their safety and happiness.

Prudence, indeed, will dictate that governments long established should not be changed for light and transient causes; and, accordingly, all experience has shown that mankind are more disposed to suffer, while evils are sufferable, than to right themselves by abolishing the forms to which they were accustomed. But when a long train of abuses and usurpations, pursuing invariably the same object, evinces a design to reduce them under absolute despotism, it is their duty to throw off such government and to provide new guards for their future security. Such has been the patient sufferance of the women under this government, and such is now the necessity which constrains them to demand the equal station to which they are entitled.

The history of mankind is a history of repeated injuries and usurpations on the part of man toward woman, having in direct object the establishment of an absolute tyranny over her. To prove this, let facts be submitted to a candid world.

He has never permitted her to exercise her inalienable right to the elective franchise.

He has compelled her to submit to laws in the formation of which she had no voice.

He has withheld from her rights which are given to the most ignorant and degraded men, both natives and foreigners.

Having deprived her of this first right of a citizen, the elective franchise, thereby leaving her without representation in the halls of legislation, he has oppressed her on all sides.

He has made her, if married, in the eye of the law, civilly dead.

He has taken from her all right in property, even to the wages she earns.

He has made her, morally, an irresponsible being, as she can commit many crimes with impunity, provided they be done in the presence of her husband. In the covenant of marriage, she is compelled to promise obedience to her husband, he becoming, to all intents and purposes, her master — the law giving him power to deprive her of her liberty and to administer chastisement.

He has so framed the laws of divorce, as to what shall be the proper causes and, in case of separation, to whom the guardianship of the children shall be given, as to be wholly regardless of the happiness of women — the law, in all cases, going upon a false supposition of the supremacy of man and giving all power into his hands.

After depriving her of all rights as a married woman, if single and the owner of property, he has taxed her to support a government which recognizes her only when her property can be made profitable to it.

He has monopolized nearly all the profitable employments, and from those she is permitted to follow, she receives but a scanty remuneration. He closes against her all the avenues to wealth and distinction which he considers most honorable to himself. As a teacher of theology, medicine, or law, she is not known.

He has denied her the facilities for obtaining a thorough education, all colleges being closed against her.

He allows her in church, as well as state, but a subordinate position, claiming apostolic authority for her exclusion from the ministry, and, with some exceptions, from any public participation in the affairs of the church.

He has created a false public sentiment by giving to the world a different code of morals for men and women, by which moral delinquencies which exclude women from society are not only tolerated but deemed of little account in man.

He has usurped the prerogative of Jehovah himself, claiming it as his right to assign for her a sphere of action, when that belongs to her conscience and to her God.

He has endeavored, in every way that he could, to destroy her confidence in her own powers, to lessen her self-respect, and to make her willing to lead a dependent and abject life.

Now, in view of this entire disfranchisement of one-half the people of this country, their social and religious degradation, in view of the unjust laws above mentioned, and because women do feel themselves aggrieved, oppressed, and fraudulently deprived of their most sacred rights, we insist that they have immediate admission to all the rights and privileges which belong to them as citizens of the United States.

In entering upon the great work before us, we anticipate no small amount of misconception, misrepresentation, and ridicule; but we shall use every instrumentality within our power to effect our object. We shall employ agents, circulate tracts, petition the state and national legislatures, and endeavor to enlist the pulpit and the press in our behalf. We hope this Convention will be followed by a series of conventions embracing every part of the country.

RESOLUTIONS

Whereas, the great precept of nature is conceded to be that "man shall pursue his own true and substantial happiness." Black-stone in his *Commentaries* remarks that this law of nature, being coeval with mankind and dictated by God himself, is, of course, superior in obligation to any other. It is binding over all the globe, in all countries and at all times; no human laws are of any validity if contrary to this, and such of them as are valid derive all their force, and all their validity, and all their authority, mediately and immediately, from this original; therefore,

Resolved, That such laws as conflict, in any way, with the true and substantial happiness of woman, are contrary to the great precept of nature and of no validity, for this is "superior in obligation to any other."

Resolved, that all laws which prevent woman from occupying such a station in society as her conscience shall dictate, or which place her in a position inferior to that of man, are contrary to the great precept of nature and therefore of no force or authority.

Resolved, that woman is man's equal, was intended to be so by the Creator, and the highest good of the race demands that she should be recognized as such.

Resolved, that the women of this country ought to be enlightened in regard to the laws under which they live, that they may no longer publish their degradation by declaring themselves satisfied with their present position, nor their ignorance, by asserting that they have all the rights they want.

Resolved, that inasmuch as man, while claiming for himself intellectual superiority, does accord to woman moral superiority, it is preeminently his duty to encourage her to speak and teach, as she has an opportunity, in all religious assemblies.

Resolved, that the same amount of virtue, delicacy, and refinement of behavior that is required of woman in the social state should also be required of man, and the same transgressions should be visited with equal severity on both man and woman.

Resolved, that the objection of indelicacy and impropriety, which is so often brought against woman when she addresses a public audience, comes with a very ill grace from those who encourage, by their attendance, her appearance on the stage, in the concert, or in feats of the circus.

Resolved, that woman has too long rested satisfied in the circumscribed limits which corrupt customs and a perverted application of the Scriptures have marked out for her, and that it is time she should move in the enlarged sphere which her great Creator has assigned her.

Resolved, that it is the duty of the women on this country to secure to themselves their sacred right to the elective franchise.

Resolved, that the equality of human rights results necessarily from the fact of the identity of the race in capabilities and responsibilities.

Resolved, that the speedy success of our cause depends upon the zealous and untiring efforts of both men and women for the overthrow of the monopoly of the pulpit, and for the securing to woman an equal participation with men in the various trades, professions, and commerce.

Resolved, *therefore*, that, being invested by the Creator with the same capabilities and the same consciousness of responsibility for their exercise, it is demonstrably the right and duty of woman, equally with man, to promote every righteous cause by every righteous means; and especially in regard to the great subjects of morals and religion, it is self-evidently her right to participate with her brother in teaching them, both in private and in public, by writing and by speaking, by any instrumentalities proper to be used, and in any assemblies proper to be held; and this being a self-evident truth growing out of the divinely implanted principles of human nature, any custom or authority adverse to it, whether modern or wearing the hoary sanction of antiquity, is to be regarded as a self-evident falsehood, and at war with mankind.

WILLIAM LLOYD GARRISON: FOR IMMEDIATE ABOLITION (1831)

Liberator, January 1, 1831.

In the month of August I issued proposals for publishing the *Liberator* in Washington City; but the enterprise, though hailed in different sections of the country, was palsied by public indifference. Since that time, the removal of the *Genius of Universal Emancipation* to the seat of government has rendered less imperious the establishment of a similar periodical in that quarter.

During my recent tour for the purpose of exciting the minds of the people by a series of discourses on the subject of slavery, every place that I visited gave fresh evidence of the fact that a greater revolution in public sentiment was to be effected in the free states — *and particularly in New England* — than at the South. I found contempt more bitter, opposition more active, detraction more relentless, prejudice more stubborn, and apathy more frozen than among slaveowners themselves. Of course, there were individual exceptions to the contrary. This state of things afflicted but did not dishearten me. I determined, at every hazard, to lift up the standard of emancipation in the eyes of the nation, *within sight of Bunker Hill and in the birthplace of liberty*. That standard is now unfurled; and long may it float, unhurt by the spoliations of time or the missiles of a desperate foe — yea, till every chain be broken and every bondman set free! Let Southern oppressors tremble; let their secret abettors tremble; let their Northern apologists tremble; let all the enemies of the persecuted blacks tremble.

I deem the publication of my original prospectus unnecessary, as it has obtained a wide circulation. The principles therein inculcated will be steadily pursued in this paper, excepting that I shall not array myself as the political partisan of any man. In defending the great cause of human rights, I wish to derive the assistance of all religions and of all parties.

Assenting to the "self-evident truth" maintained in the American Declaration of Independence, "that all men are created equal and endowed by their Creator with certain inalienable rights, among which are life, liberty, and the pursuit of happiness," I shall strenuously contend for the immediate enfranchisement of our slave population. In Park Street Church, on the Fourth of July, 1829, in an address on slavery, I unreflectingly assented to the popular but pernicious doctrine of *gradual* abolition. I seize this opportunity to make a full and unequivocal recantation, and thus publicly to ask pardon of my God, of my country, and of my brethren, the poor slaves, for having uttered a sentiment so full of timidity, injustice, and absurdity. A similar recantation from my pen was published in the *Genius of Universal Emancipation* at Baltimore, in September 1829. My conscience is now satisfied.

I am aware that many object to the severity of my language; but is there not cause for severity? I *will be* as harsh as truth and as uncompromising as justice. On this subject I do not wish to think, or speak, or write with moderation. No! No! Tell a man whose house is on fire to give a moderate alarm; tell him to moderately rescue his wife from the hands of the ravisher; tell the mother to gradually extricate her babe from the fire into which it has fallen—but urge me not to use moderation in a cause like the present. I am in earnest; I will not equivocate; I will not excuse; I will not retreat a single inch—AND I WILL BE HEARD. The apathy of the people is enough to make every statue leap from its pedestal and to hasten the resurrection of the dead.

It is pretended that I am retarding the cause of emancipation by the coarseness

of my invective and the precipitancy of my measures. *The charge is not true.* On this question my influence, humble as it is, is felt at this moment to a considerable extent, and shall be felt in coming years—not perniciously but beneficially: not as a curse but as a blessing—and posterity will bear testimony that I was right. I desire to thank God that He enables me to disregard "the fear of man which bringeth a snare," and to speak His truth in its simplicity and power.

JOHN L. O'SULLIVAN: OUR MANIFEST DESTINY (1845)

United States Magazine and Democratic Review, July 1845: "Annexation."

It is time now for opposition to the annexation of Texas to cease, all further agitation of the waters of bitterness and strife, at least in connection with this question, even though it may perhaps be required of us as a necessary condition of the freedom of our institutions, that we must live on forever in a state of unpausing struggle and excitement upon some subject of party division or other. But, in regard to Texas, enough has now been given to party. It is time for the common duty of patriotism to the country to succeed; or if this claim will not be recognized, it is at least time for common sense to acquiesce with decent grace in the inevitable and the irrevocable.

Texas is now ours. Already, before these words are written, her convention has undoubtedly ratified the acceptance, by her congress, of our proffered invitation into the Union; and made the requisite changes in her already republican form of constitution to adapt it to its future federal relations. Her star and her stripe may already be said to have taken their place in the glorious blazon of our common nationality; and the sweep of our eagle's wing already includes within its circuit the wide extent of her fair and fertile land.

She is no longer to us a mere geographical space — a certain combination of coast, plain, mountain, valley, forest, and stream. She is no longer to us a mere country on the map. She comes within the dear and sacred designation of our country; no longer a *pays* [country], she is a part of *la patrie*; and that which is at once a sentiment and a virtue, patriotism, already begins to thrill for her too within the national heart.

It is time then that all should cease to treat her as alien, and even adverse — cease to denounce and vilify all and everything connected with her accession — cease to thwart and oppose the remaining steps for its consummation; or where such efforts are felt to be unavailing, at least to embitter the hour of reception by all the most ungracious frowns of aversion and words of unwelcome. There has been enough of all this. It has had its fitting day during the period when, in common with every other possible question of practical policy that can arise, it unfortunately became one of the leading topics of party division, of presidential electioneering.

But that period has passed, and with it let its prejudices and its passions, its discords and its denunciations, pass away too. The next session of Congress will see the representatives of the new young state in their places in both our halls of national legislation, side by side with those of the old Thirteen. Let their reception into "the family" be frank, kindly, and cheerful, as befits such an occasion, as comports not less with our own self-respect than patriotic duty towards them. Ill betide those foul birds that delight to file their own nest, and disgust the ear with perpetual discord of illomened croak.

Why, were other reasoning wanting, in favor of now elevating this question of the reception of Texas into the Union, out of the lower region of our past party dissensions, up to its proper level of a high and broad nationality, it surely is to be found, found abundantly, in the manner in which other nations have undertaken to intrude themselves into it, between us and the proper parties to the case, in a spirit of hostile interference against us, for the avowed object of thwarting our policy and hampering our power, limiting our greatness and checking the fulfillment of our manifest destiny to overspread the continent allotted by Providence for the free development of our yearly multiplying millions. This we have seen done by England, our old rival and enemy; and by France, strangely coupled with her against us, under the influence of the Anglicism strongly tinging the policy of her present prime minister, Guizot.

The zealous activity with which this effort to defeat us was pushed by the representatives of those governments, together with the character of intrigue accompanying it, fully constituted that case of foreign interference, which Mr. Clay himself declared should, and would unite us all in maintaining the common cause of our country against the foreigner and the foe. We are only astonished that this effect has not been more fully and strongly produced, and that the burst of indignation against this unauthorized, insolent, and hostile interference against us, has not been more general even among the party before opposed to annexation, and has not rallied the national spirit and national pride unanimously upon that policy. We are very sure that if Mr. Clay himself were now to add another letter to his former Texas correspondence, he would express this sentiment, and carry out the idea already strongly stated in one of them, in a manner which would tax all the powers of blushing belonging to some of his party adherents.

It is wholly untrue, and unjust to ourselves, the pretense that the annexation has been a measure of spoliation, unrightful and unrighteous—of military conquest under forms of peace and law—of territorial aggrandizement at the expense of justice, and justice due by a double sanctity to the weak. This view of the question is wholly unfounded, and has been before so amply refuted in these pages, as well as in a thousand other modes, that we shall not again dwell upon it.

The independence of Texas was complete and absolute. It was an independence, not only in fact, but of right.

No obligation of duty toward Mexico tended in the least degree to restrain our right to effect the desired recovery of the fair province once our own—whatever motives of policy might have prompted a more deferential consideration of her feelings and her pride, as involved in the question. If Texas became peopled with an American population, it was by no contrivance of our government, but on the express invitation of that of Mexico herself; accompanied with such guaranties of state independence, and the maintenance of a federal system analogous to our own, as constituted a compact fully justifying the strongest measures of redress on the part of those afterward deceived in this guaranty, and sought to be enslaved under the yoke imposed by its violation.

She was released, rightfully and absolutely released, from all Mexican allegiance, or duty of cohesion to the Mexican political body, by the acts and fault of Mexico herself, and Mexico alone. There never was a clearer case. It was not revolution; it was resistance to revolution: and resistance under such circumstances as left independence the necessary resulting state, caused by the abandonment of those with whom her former federal association had existed. What then can be more preposterous than all this clamor by Mexico and the Mexican interest, against annexation, as a violation of any rights of hers, any duties of ours?...

Nor is there any just foundation for the charge that annexation is a great pro-slavery measure—calculated to increase and perpetuate that institution. Slavery had nothing to do with it. Opinions were and are greatly divided, both at the North and South, as to the influence to be exerted by it on slavery and the slave states. That it will tend to facilitate and hasten the disappearance of slavery from all the northern tier of the present slave states, cannot surely admit of serious question. The greater value in Texas of the slave labor now employed in those states, must soon produce the effect of draining off that labor southwardly, by the same unvarying law that bids water descend the slope that invites it.

Every new slave state in Texas will make at least one free state from among those in which that institution now exists—to say nothing of those portions of Texas on which slavery cannot spring and grow—to say nothing of the far more rapid growth of new states in the free West and Northwest, as these fine regions are overspread by the emigration fast flowing over them from Europe, as well as from the Northern and Eastern states of the Union as it exists. On the other hand, it is undeniably much gained for the cause of the eventual voluntary abolition of slavery, that it should have been thus drained off toward the only outlet which appeared to furnish much probability of the ultimate disappearance of the Negro race from our borders.

The Spanish-Indian-American populations of Mexico, Central America, and South America, afford the only receptacle capable of absorbing that race whenever we shall be prepared to slough it off—to emancipate it from slavery, and (simultaneously necessary) to remove it from the midst of our own. Themselves already of mixed and confused blood, and free from the "prejudices" which among us so insuperably forbid the social amalgamation which can alone elevate the Negro race out of a virtually servile degradation; even though legally free the regions occupied by those populations must strongly attract the black race in that direction; and as soon as the destined hour of emancipation shall arrive, will relieve the question of one of its worst difficulties, if not absolutely the greatest....

California will, probably, next fall away from the loose adhesion which, in such a country as Mexico, holds a remote province in a slight equivocal kind of dependence on the metropolis. Imbecile and distracted, Mexico never can exert any real government authority over such a country. The impotence of the one and the distance of the other, must make the relation one of virtual independence; unless, by stunting the province of all natural growth, and forbidding that immigration which can alone develope its capabilities and fulfill the purposes of its creation, tyranny may retain a military dominion, which is no government in the legitimate sense of the term.

In the case of California this is now impossible. The Anglo-Saxon foot is already on its borders. Already the advance guard of the irresistible army of Anglo-Saxon emigration has begun to pour down upon it, armed with the plough and the rifle, and marking its trail with schools and colleges, courts and representative halls, mills and meetinghouses. A population will soon be in actual occupation of California, over which it will be idle for Mexico to dream of dominion. They will necessarily become independent. All this without agency of our government, without responsibility of our people—in the natural flow of events, the spontaneous working of principles, and the adaptation of the tendencies and wants of the human race to the elemental circumstances in the midst of which they find themselves placed.

And they will have a right to independence—to self-government—to the possession of the homes conquered from the wilderness by their own labors and dangers, sufferings and sacrifices—a better and a truer right than the artificial title of sovereignty in Mexico, a thousand miles distant, inheriting from Spain a title good only against those who have none better. Their right to independence will be the natural right of self-government belonging to any community strong enough to maintain it—istinct in position, origin and character, and free from any mutual obligations of membership of a common political body, binding it to others by the duty of loyalty and compact of public faith. This will be their title to independence; and by this title, there can be no doubt that the population now fast streaming down upon California will both assert and maintain that independence.

Whether they will then attach themselves to our Union or not, is not to be predicted with any certainty. Unless the projected railroad across the continent to the Pacific be carried into effect, perhaps they may not; though even in that case, the day is not distant when the empires of the Atlantic and Pacific would again flow together into one, as soon as their inland border should approach each other. But that great work, colossal as appears the plan on its first suggestion, cannot remain long unbuilt.

Its necessity for this very purpose of binding and holding together in its iron clasp our fast-settling Pacific region with that of the Mississippi Valley—the natural facility of the route—the ease with which any amount of labor for the construction can be drawn in from the overcrowded populations of Europe, to be paid in the lands made valuable by the progress of the work itself—and its immense utility to the commerce of the world with the whole eastern coast of Asia, alone almost sufficient for the support of such a road—these considerations give assurance that the day cannot be distant which shall witness the conveyance of the representatives from Oregon and California to Washington within less time than a few years ago was devoted to a similar journey by those from Ohio; while the magnetic telegraph will enable the editors of the *San Francisco Union*, the *Astoria Evening Post*, or the *Nootka Morning News*, to set up in type the first half of the President's inaugural before the echoes of the latter half shall have died away beneath the lofty porch of the Capitol, as spoken from his lips.

Away, then, with all idle French talk of balances of power on the American Continent. There is no growth in Spanish America! Whatever progress of population there may be in the British Canadas, is only for their own early severance of their present colonial relation to the little island 3,000 miles across the Atlantic; soon to be followed by annexation, and destined to swell the still accumulating momentum of our progress.

And whosoever may hold the balance, though they should cast into the opposite scale all the bayonets and cannon, not only of France and England, but of Europe entire, how would it kick the beam against the simple, solid weight of the 250, or 300 million—and American millions—destined to gather beneath the flutter of the stripes and stars, in the fast hastening year of the Lord 1945!

ANDREW JACKSON: ON INDIAN REMOVAL (1830)

A Compilation of the Messages and Papers of the Presidents 1789-1897, James D. Richardson, ed., Washington, 1896-99, Vol. II, pp. 500–529.

It gives me pleasure to announce to Congress that the benevolent policy of the government, steadily pursued for nearly thirty years, in relation to the removal of the Indians beyond the white settlements is approaching to a happy consummation. Two important tribes have accepted the provision made for their removal at the last session of Congress, and it is believed that their example will induce the remaining tribes also to seek the same obvious advantages.

The consequences of a speedy removal will be important to the United States, to individual states, and to the Indians themselves. The pecuniary advantages which it promises to the government are the least of its recommendations. It puts an end to all possible danger of collision between the authorities of the general and state governments on account of the Indians. It will place a dense and civilized population in large tracts of country now occupied by a few savage hunters. By opening the whole territory between Tennessee on the north and Louisiana on the south to the settlement of the whites it will incalculably strengthen the southwestern frontier and render the adjacent states strong enough to repel future invasions without remote aid. It will relieve the whole state of Mississippi and the western part of Alabama of Indian occupancy, and enable those states to advance rapidly in population, wealth, and power.

It will separate the Indians from immediate contact with settlements of whites; free them from the power of the states; enable them to pursue happiness in their own way and under their own rude institutions; will retard the progress of decay, which is lessening their numbers, and perhaps cause them gradually, under the protection of the government and through the influence of good counsels, to cast off their savage habits and become an interesting, civilized, and Christian community. These consequences, some of them so certain and the rest so prob-able, make the complete execution of the plan sanctioned by Congress at their last session an object of much solicitude.

Toward the aborigines of the coun-try no one can indulge a more friendly feeling than myself, or would go further in attempting to reclaim them from their wandering habits and make them a happy, prosperous people. I have endeavored to impress upon them my own solemn convictions of the duties and powers of the general government in relation to the state authorities. For the justice of the laws passed by the states within the scope of their reserved powers they are not responsible to this government. As individuals we may entertain and express our opinions of their acts, but as a gov-ernment we have as little right to control them as we have to prescribe laws for other nations.

With a full understanding of the subject, the Choctaw and the Chickasaw tribes have with great unanimity deter-mined to avail themselves of the liberal offers presented by the act of Congress, and have agreed to remove beyond the Mississippi River. Treaties have been made with them, which in due season will be submitted for consideration. In nego-tiating these treaties, they were made to understand their true condition, and they have preferred maintaining their independence in the Western forests to submitting to the laws of the states in which they now reside. These treaties, being probably the last which will ever be made with them, are characterized by

great liberality on the part of the govern-ment. They give the Indians a liberal sum in consideration of their removal, and comfortable subsistence on their arrival at their new homes. If it be their real interest to maintain a separate existence, they will there be at liberty to do so with-out the inconveniences and vexations to which they would unavoidably have been subject in Alabama and Mississippi.

Humanity has often wept over the fate of the aborigines of this country, and philanthropy has been long busily employed in devising means to avert it, but its progress has never for a moment been arrested, and one by one have many powerful tribes disappeared from the earth. To follow to the tomb the last of his race and to tread on the graves of extinct nations excite melancholy reflections. But true philanthropy reconciles the mind to these vicissitudes as it does to the extinction of one generation to make room for another. In the monuments and fortresses of an unknown people, spread over the extensive regions of the West, we behold the memorials of a once powerful race, which was exterminated or has dis-appeared to make room for the existing savage tribes. Nor is there anything in this which, upon a comprehensive view of the general interests of the human race, is to be regretted. Philanthropy could not wish to see this continent restored to the condition in which it was found by our forefathers. What good man would prefer a country covered with forests and ranged by a few thousand sav-ages to our extensive republic, studded with cities, towns, and prosperous farms, embellished with all the improvements which art can devise or industry execute, occupied by more than 12 million happy people, and filled with all the blessings of liberty, civilization, and religion?

The present policy of the government is but a continuation of the same progressive change by a milder process. The tribes which occupied the countries now constituting the Eastern states were annihilated or have melted away to make room for the whites. The waves of population and civilization are rolling to the westward, and we now propose to acquire the countries occupied by the red men of the South and West by a fair exchange, and, at the expense of the United States, to send them to a land where their existence may be prolonged and perhaps made perpetual.

Doubtless it will be painful to leave the graves of their fathers; but what do they more than our ancestors did or than our children are now doing? To better their condition in an unknown land our forefathers left all that was dear in earthly objects. Our children by thousands yearly leave the land of their birth to seek new homes in distant regions. Does humanity weep at these painful separations from everything, animate and inanimate, with which the young heart has become entwined? Far from it. It is rather a source of joy that our country affords scope where our young population may range unconstrained in body or in mind, developing the power and faculties of man in their highest perfection. These remove

hundreds and almost thousands of miles at their own expense, purchase the lands they occupy, and support themselves at their new homes from the moment of their arrival. Can it be cruel in this government when, by events which it cannot control, the Indian is made discontented in his ancient home to purchase his lands, to give him a new and extensive territory, to pay the expense of his removal, and support him a year in his new abode? How many thousands of our own people would gladly embrace the opportunity of removing to the West on such conditions? If the offers made to the Indians were extended to them, they would be hailed with gratitude and joy.

And is it supposed that the wandering savage has a stronger attachment to his home than the settled, civilized Christian? Is it more afflicting to him to leave the graves of his fathers than it is to our brothers and children? Rightly considered, the policy of the general government toward the red man is not only liberal but generous. He is unwilling to submit to the laws of the states and mingle with their population. To save him from this alternative, or perhaps utter annihilation, the general government kindly offers him a new home, and proposes to pay the whole expense of his removal and settlement.

In the consummation of a policy originating at an early period, and steadily pursued by every administration within the present century—so just to the states and so generous to the Indians—the executive feels it has a right to expect the cooperation of Congress and of all good and disinterested men. The states, moreover, have a right to demand it. It was substantially a part of the compact which made them members of our Confederacy. With Georgia there is an express contract; with the new states an implied one of equal obligation. Why, in authorizing Ohio, Indiana, Illinois, Missouri, Mississippi, and Alabama to form constitutions and become separate states, did Congress include within their limits extensive tracts of Indian lands, and, in some instances, powerful Indian tribes? Was it not understood by both parties that the power of the states was to be coextensive with their limits, and that, with all convenient dispatch, the general government should extinguish the Indian title and remove every obstruction to the complete jurisdiction of the state governments over the soil? Probably not one of those states would have accepted a separate existence—certainly it would never have been granted by Congress—had it been understood that they were to be confined forever to those small portions of their nominal territory the Indian title to which had at the time been extinguished.

It is, therefore, a duty which this government owes to the new states to extinguish as soon as possible the Indian title to all lands which Congress themselves have included within their limits. When this is done the duties of the general government in relation to the states and the Indians within their limits are at an end. The Indians may leave the state

or not, as they choose. The purchase of their lands does not alter in the least their personal relations with the state government. No act of the general government has ever been deemed necessary to give the states jurisdiction over the persons of the Indians. That they possess by virtue of their sovereign power within their own limits in as full a manner before as after the purchase of the Indian lands; nor can this government add to or diminish it.

May we not hope, therefore, that all good citizens, and none more zealously than those who think the Indians oppressed by subjection to the laws of the states, will unite in attempting to open the eyes of those children of the forest to their true condition, and by a speedy removal to relieve them from all the evils, real or imaginary, present or prospective, with which they may be supposed to be threatened.

TERRITORIAL EXPANSION AND THE EXTENSION OF SLAVERY (1847)

United States Magazine and Democratic Review, October 1847: "New Territory versus No Territory."

The war, which the insane folly of the Spaniards has forced upon us after fifty years of threatening and surrendering of territory reluctantly as we have pressed upon their front, has the disadvantage of acquiring territory too fast, "before our population is sufficiently advanced to gain it from them piece by piece." That was a wise policy ascribed in the early stages of the war to Almonte and his party, who, learning more from the experience of the past than our own politicians have done, saw in the last fifty years of peace the steady and resistless approach of the American people. They saw territory after territory, no matter by whom owned or by what people inhabited, swallowed up in the great Union, the march of which was not perceptibly stayed, even when Louisiana and its French citizens became an American republic. They saw Texas suddenly grow into a state through Anglo-Saxon energy, and as promptly fall into the line of the Union, while its pioneers were already taking root in California and New Mexico.

The "coquetry" of the Texan rulers with Great Britain and Mexico was not more successful than that of former similar attempts; and Captain Elliot won no more fame than Arbuthnot in Florida, Powers in Kentucky, or Germaine in Vermont. If ten years sufficed to swallow up Texas, as many more would involve a province in Mexico, and to this progress an obstinate war might be a barrier. But alas! their power to resist an American Army was less even than their ability to resist the approach of settlers. The occupation of their soil by volunteer troops, who are precisely the most enterprising class of a race unequaled for energy, only clears the way for the no less adventurous settlers. The 30,000 intelligent men who visit the admirable climate, fertile fields, and boundless mineral resources of Mexico will at least familiarize the minds of the people at home with the advantages there offered and possibly stimulate the emigration.

It matters not whether a treaty stipulates for more or less territory, it will all come into the country "piece by piece" as "our population are sufficiently advanced to gain it." The surrender of Texas by the Treaty of 1819 was fondly hoped by the "No Territory" Party to have put that matter at rest, and no doubt many a purblind Federalist looked upon the Sabine as the utmost southern limit of the Union. That dishonorable dismemberment, however, has brought its own punishment in the pretext it offered the Spaniards for an attack which must end in a removal of the boundary still farther south and a completion of its western progress.

This occupation of territory by the people is the great movement of the age, and until every acre of the North American continent is occupied by citizens of the United States, the foundation of the future empire will not have been laid. The chief evil of Europe, that which oppresses England and destroys Ireland, is the exclusion of the people from the soil. England, with a population larger than our Union, has but 32,000 proprietors of the soil. That which constitutes the strength of the Union, the wealth and independence of its people, is the boundless expanse of territory laid open to their possession; and the more rapidly it is overrun by needy settlers, the greater is the security that it will be equally and extensively distributed, and the more impossible it becomes for any section or clique to exercise "control over them," or to encroach upon the rights they enjoy under our Constitution.

All the territory of the Union is the common property of all the states—every member, new or old, of the Union, admitted to partnership under the Constitution, has a perfect right to enjoy the territory, which is the common property of all. Some of the territory was acquired by treaty from England; much of it by cession from the older states; yet more by treaties with Indians, and still greater quantities by purchase from Spain and France; large tracts again by the annexation of Texas; and the present war will add still more to the quantity yet to be entered by citizens of the United States, or of those of any of the countries of Europe that choose to migrate thither.

All this land, no matter whence it was derived, belongs to all the states jointly. That acquired from England by treaty was in their joint capacity as a federal government; that purchased from Indians and foreign governments was paid for with the money drawn through customs duties from the citizens of all the states; and funds derived from those sources, backed by blood drawn mostly from the South, is the price paid for conquered territory; and no citizen of the United States can be debarred from moving thither with his property and enjoying the liberties guaranteed by the Constitution.

The lands ceded to the United States collectively, by individual states that claimed them, were accepted by acts of Congress that specified "that no regulations made or to be made by Congress shall tend to emancipate slaves." The right of all the citizens of the older states to emigrate with all their property whatsoever, and enjoy therewith the vacant lands, is perfect. The instrument by which the thirteen original slave states entered into a union which admitted Vermont as a slave state recognizes and guarantees slaves as the property of their owners. That instrument expressly allowed the importation of slaves into the Union until 1808, at a duty not to exceed $10 per head; and Section 2, Article IV, providing for the recovery of fugitive slaves from labor, manifestly admits and asserts the exercise of a positive, unqualified right on the part of the owner of the slave, which no state law or regulation can in any way qualify, regulate, control, or restrain.

Any law or regulation which interrupts, limits, delays or postpones the rights of the owner to the immediate command of his service or labor, operates a discharge of the slave from service, and is a violation of the Constitution. This right of property in slaves is guaranteed as a municipal regulation; it in no shape bears a national character under the Constitution, and the original states enjoyed that property as long as it was profitable to them. When it ceased to be so, some of them abolished the institution without reference to the federal government. It was a species of property that they had a right to sell elsewhere or relinquish at their pleasure. Other states, however, are yet in possession of that property as well as their rights in the new territory. To set up, therefore, a pretense that if they adhere to the property they possess they shall be deprived of their rights in the states to be formed in any acquired territory is an unprincipled violation of a solemn treaty, an attack upon the Constitution, and a gross injustice to the rights of neighboring states.

If the Constitution is respected, then the rights of no member in the common property can be impaired, because it is possessed of other property distasteful to other members. If the Constitution is not respected, then the right of one state to interfere with the internal affairs of another is no greater than to meddle with serfdom in Russia or slavery in India. Unfortunately, this institution in the South, once common to all the states, has on several occasions received somewhat of a national character, particularly in the Missouri Compromise, where a line of latitude was fixed to the north of which no slave state should be erected; and, on several other occasions, in a less marked manner. It is, therefore, the more necessary that its purely municipal character should be distinctly borne in mind, and that it should not be permitted to be used as a means of checking the expansion of the Union by preventing any description of emigrants from occupying any territory best suited to their means and interests....

The whole tendency of these attempts to enforce, through conditions of admission into the Union, a control over the states by Congress, not authorized by the Constitution, is dangerously and illegally to enlarge the powers of the federal government and produce inequality among the states. The Constitution does not prohibit slavery in any of the states, and, yet, through the Missouri Compromise, it is sought to usurp for Congress the power to prohibit it in a number of states that will hereafter grow up. When these new states come into the Union, they are controlled by the Constitution only; and as that instrument permits slavery in all the states that are parties to it, how can Congress prevent it? To attempt it is clearly such a departure from the spirit of the Constitution as is at war with the whole course of the Democratic Party, and as such cannot have a prosperous issue.

That the question of slavery—a purely municipal matter and, as such, entirely without the range of congressional control—has, unfortunately, on more than one occasion, approached a national form by being made the subject of official documents, not in defense of any foreign aggression upon our domestic rights is matter of regret; but does not, therefore, confer the right to confirm that national appearance by national action. On the other hand, it calls for a more rigid acknowledgment of the immunities due to each member of the Union, present and to come.

A great deal of controversy seems to arise from misunderstanding, as thus: One party states that "if territory is to be conquered or purchased *for the purpose* of extending slavery," it is a violation of the Constitution. Nothing can be more clear. But when, through the results of war, territory comes into the possession of the Union, it is equally a violation of the Constitution for Congress to undertake to say that there shall be no slavery then. The people of the United States were nearly unanimous for the admission of Texas into the Union; but probably not an insignificant fraction required its annexation *"for the purpose"* of extending slavery.

The acquirement of territory by Congress is in accordance with the policy of the Union, but no more "for the purpose of extending slavery" than for the extension of Mormonism, or any sect of religion or school of philosophy. There is a vast distinction between "annexation for the purpose of extending slavery" and making the exclusion of slavery the condition of annexation; both are equally at war with the Constitution, which permits the acquirement of territory but forbids meddling with slavery, pro or con.

accede To give in to a request or demand.

ad valorem Imposed at a rate percent of value.

antebellum Existing before the American Civil War.

beshrew Curse.

bumptiousness The quality or state of being presumptuously, obtusely, and often noisily self-assertive.

cisatlantic Of, relating to, or characteristic of the side of the Atlantic Ocean regarded as the near side.

eleemosynary Of, relating to, or supported by charity.

ephemeral Lasting a very short time.

exceptionalism A theory expounding the conditions that set apart a nation or region from the norm.

exchequer Treasury, especially a national or royal treasury.

Federalist Party Early U.S. national political party, which advocated a strong central government.

fetter Something that confines; restraint.

Fourierism A philosophy of social reform developed by Charles Fourier that advocated transforming society into cooperative communities of small self-sustaining groups.

franchise The right to vote.

freehold Ownership of real estate.

grandiloquent Characterized by lofty, extravagantly colourful, pompous, or bombastic style, manner, or quality especially in language.

hinterland A region lying beyond major metropolitan or cultural centres.

impolitic Untactful or unwise.

inculcate To teach and impress by frequent repetitions or admonitions.

interdict To forbid in a usually formal or authoritative manner.

invidious Of an unpleasant or objectionable nature.

junto A group of persons joined for a common purpose.

manifest destiny A future event viewed as inevitable; an ostensibly benevolent or necessary policy of imperialistic expansion.

millennialism Belief in the one-thousand-year period mentioned in Revelation 20 during which holiness is to prevail and Christ is to reign on earth.

nullification The action of a state impeding or attempting to prevent the operation and enforcement within its territory of a law of the United States.

pauper One who receives aid from funds designated for the poor.

pecuniary Consisting of or measured in money.

penny press A tabloid newspaper popular in the 19th century because of its low price (usually a penny).

perfidy The quality or state of being faithless or disloyal.

perspicuity The quality or state of being plain to the understanding especially because of clarity and precision of presentation.

pet bank Any of a group of state banks selected as depositories of federal funds removed from the United States Bank during the first Jacksonian administration.

plebeian Crude or coarse in manner or style; common.

plum Something desirable given in return for a favour.

precisianism The practice of scrupulous adherence to a strict standard especially of religious observance or morality.

preponderating Preponderant, excessive in influence, power, or importance.

procurement The obtaining of military supplies by a government.

proletarian The lowest social or economic class of a community; the industrial labouring class.

purblind Lacking in vision, insight, or understanding; obtuse.

remonstrance An earnest presentation of reasons for opposition or grievance.

salutatory An address or statement of welcome or greeting.

scion A detached living portion of a plant (as a bud or shoot) joined to a stock in grafting and usually supplying solely aerial parts to a graft.

solicitude An attitude of earnest concern or attention.

spoils system A practice of regarding public offices and their emoluments as plunder to be distributed to members of the victorious party.

totalitarian Of or relating to centralized control by an autocratic leader or hierarchy.

wanderlust Strong longing for or impulse toward wandering.

windjammer A sailing ship.

yeomanry The body of small landed proprietors of the middle class.

BIBLIOGRAPHY

THE ERA OF MIXED FEELINGS

Sean Wilentz, *The Rise of American Democracy: Jefferson to Lincoln* (2005), provides great insight into this period, as does George Dangerfield, *The Era of Good Feelings* (1952, reprinted 1973). Shaw Livermore, Jr., *The Twilight of Federalism: The Disintegration of the Federalist Party, 1815–1830* (1962, reissued 1972), is an excellent analysis.

ECONOMIC DEVELOPMENT

Valuable and informative are Seth Rockman, *Scraping By* (2009); Charles Sellers, *The Market Revolution: Jacksonian America, 1815–1846* (1991); and Edward Pessen, *Most Uncommon Jacksonians: The Radical Leaders of the Early Labor Movement* (1967, reprinted 1970).

AFRICAN AMERICAN LIFE, SLAVERY, AND ABOLITIONISM

Particularly noteworthy studies are Walter Johnson, *Soul by Soul* (1999); John Stauffer, *The Black Hearts of Men* (2004); Charles Joyner, *Down by the Riverside*, 25th anniversary ed. (2009); Eugene D. Genovese, *Roll, Jordan, Roll: The World the Slaves Made* (1974); and Herbert G. Gutman, *The Black Family in Slavery and Freedom, 1750–1925* (1976).

SOCIAL AND INTELLECTUAL DEVELOPMENTS

Lightly documented but brilliantly insightful is Alexis de Tocqueville, *Democracy in America*, 2 vol. (1835; originally published in French, 1835), available in many later editions. Edward Pessen, *Riches, Class, and Power Before the Civil War* (1973), challenges Tocqueville's version of equality in Jacksonian America. Other useful treatments are Sean Wilentz and Jonathan Earle (eds.), *Major Problems of the Early Republic*, 2nd ed. (2008); Paul E. Johnson, *A Shopkeeper's Millennium: Society and Revivals in Rochester, New York, 1815–37*, rev. ed (2004); Jonathan Daniel Wells, *The Origins of the Southern Middle Class, 1800–1860* (2004); William H. Pease and Jane H. Pease, *The Web of Progress: Private Values and Public Styles in Boston and Charleston, 1828–1843* (1985); and Barbara Welter, *Dimity Convictions: The American Woman in the Nineteenth Century* (1976). Joel Myerson, Sandra Harbert Petrulionis, and Laura Dassow Walls (eds.), *The Oxford Handbook of Transcendentalism* (2010); Joel Myerson (ed). *Transcendentalism: A Reader* (2000); and Lawrence Buell, *New England Literary Culture: From Revolution Through Renaissance* (1986), provide valuable introductions to Transcendentalism and the literature of New England during this period.

JACKSONIAN POLITICS

Very useful is Harry L. Watson, *Liberty and Power: The Politics of Jacksonian America*, rev. ed. (2006). Arthur M. Schlesinger, Jr., *The Age of Jackson* (1945, reissued 1953), is an influential study that stimulated a great array of refutations of its pro-Jackson interpretation, including Edward Pessen, *Jacksonian America*, new ed. (1978, reprinted 1985). A stimulating if not always convincing comparison of Jacksonian and earlier America is Robert H. Wiebe, *The Opening of American Society: From the Adoption of the Constitution to the Eve of Disunion* (1984). Richard P. McCormick, *The Second American Party System* (1966, reissued 1973), is an influential study. Michael Paul Rogin, *Fathers and Children: Andrew Jackson and the Subjugation of the American Indian* (1975), is brilliant, original, and controversial. John M. Belohlavek, *Let the Eagle Soar!: The Foreign Policy of Andrew Jackson* (1985), fills a void in the Jacksonian literature.

EXPANSIONISM

Bernard De Voto, *The Year of Decision, 1846* (1942, reissued 1989); and K. Jack Bauer, *The Mexican War, 1846–1848* (1974), are scholarly treatments.